THE FICTION OF ERNEST HEMINGWAY

N.G. MESHRAM

ATLANTIC
PUBLISHERS & DISTRIBUTORS (P) LTD

ATLANTIC
PUBLISHERS & DISTRIBUTORS (P) LTD
7/22, Ansari Road, Darya Ganj, New Delhi
Tel.: +91-11-4077 5252, 2327 3880
E-mail: orders@atlanticbooks.com
Web: www.atlanticbooks.com

Published by Atlantic Publishers & Distributors (P) Ltd 2024

Printed & bound in India by Atlantic Print Services

DEDICATED TO

My Parents

Late Gopal and Late Jamuna

Writing, at its best, is a lonely life. Organisations for writers palliate the writer's loneliness but I doubt if they improve his writing. He grows in public stature as he sheds his loneliness and often his work deteriorates. For he does his work alone and if he is a good enough writer he must face eternity, or the lack of it, each day.

For a true writer, each book should be a new beginning where he tries again for something that is beyond attainment. He should always try for something that has never been done or that others have tried and failed. Then sometimes, with great luck, he will succeed.

How simple the writing of literature would be if it were only necessary to write in another way what has been well written. It is because we have had such great writers in the past that a writer is driven far out past where he can go, out to where no one can help him.

I have spoken too long for a writer. A writer should write what he has to say and not speak it.

(Excerpts from Hemingway's Nobel Prize acceptance speech read in his absence by John C. Cabot., the then united states Ambassador to Sweden.)

Preface

My approach to literature is rather unconventional. A literary text does not appeal to me if it does not contain social significance. Even Shakespeare fails to appeal me because his so-called larger human understanding fails to touch the social issues like race and gender, though, of course Shakespeare was very much a man of his own time. Ernest Hemingway has always been presented by the critics as an artist with a gender bias. To me this opinion is incorrect. I find Hemingway's artistic vision large enough to include a sympathetic view of a woman. This I have elaborated lucidly in the book. I found in Hemingway a deep concern for the plight of the common man who was awakened to bitter realities after the World War I. Hemingway could have chosen elite issues for his fiction as most of the modernist novelists in Europe and America did. He, however, chose to write about the common man who was the worst victim of the war. This is one reason why I am invariably drawn towards the Hemingway fiction.

Most of the critics and scholars have studied Hemingway as a modernist writer with the elitist concept of man. My understanding of Hemingway as an artist differs from those of the established scholars. I found him as an artist with broader vision of man and the universe. Though he is a writer mostly down-to-earth, he can soar high in the realm of divine love.

This is more explicit in his later novels published posthumously. His sympathy for women and even support to their cause became the subject matter of his later novels. I have tried to explore this and project it in this study.

I sincerely thank Dr. R.J. Bhongle, Professor and Head of the Department of English, Mumbai University for his valuable guidance, co-operation and encouragement in writing of this book.

My thanks are due also to my wife Pushpa, daughters Mallika and Kanika and son Sidharth for their co-operation and active help during the course of my study and in making this publication possible. My sincere thanks are also due to Dr. K.R. Gupta of M/s Atlantic Publishers and Distributors, New Delhi for showing his keen interest in the subject of this book and for his efforts in bringing out this book at a proper time.

N.G. MESHRAM

Contents

1

IN HIS TIMES: AMERICA IN 1920S—A SOCIO-CULTURAL BACKGROUND TO HEMINGWAY'S FICTION

The history of American fiction is a steady progress towards realism. The hazy and mysterious atmosphere in the novels of Hawthorne and Melville was replaced by the stark social realism of Mark Twain, which, again, gave in to the new social realism of 1890s. The naturalist novel of this decade resulted straightway into the modernist novel of the early decades of twentieth century. The origin of modernism in America lies in the last decade of 19th century. The factors, which contributed to modernity in literature, or to the "modernist sensibility" in America, of which Ernest Hemingway is the finest example, began to occur immediately after the civil war.

The last two decades of 19th century in Europe as well as in America were decades of large intellectual changes. The American society, in particular, moved in the direction of technolization, urbanization, and secularization, which, ultimately resulted in modernization. The process is so closely linked with the American society that modernization and Americanization are often considered as synonymous. It was an ideological change because American society had to alter the earlier policies and ideologies so that new America was born. As a critic suggested, America was born in the country and moved into the city.[1]

The old agrarian society was transformed into the industrial one. It was a move from homestead to small town and to the city. In demography (study of the statistics of birth, death, disease etc.), it has to deal with population explosion vastly exploded by immigration and focused in cities like Chicago, New York etc. Culturally, it was the breakdown of Boston as a center of cultural and intellectual activities. The Americans also witnessed and accepted the new world-view more secular and scientific than the previous one which was Puritan and based on Christianity. All this reflected in literature of the time. The general world-view prevalent at this time in America is summed up in literature by the term "naturalism" which explains the nature of relationship between man and nature and the social factors, which surround the life of an individual. Naturalism is the late 19th-century American literature became an inevitable trait of the 20th-century modernism. It also led way up to the truly native literature in America. The cultural 'self-reliance,' which was so fondly discussed and desired by the 19th-century thinkers like Emerson, and emerged in the works of poets like Whitman, was prominently felt in America during 1920s. This decade is remarkable not only because it provided all time literary classics, but also because it was the most critical phase in American history, as indeed, in the history of entire West. Unforeseen problems in a variety of manners now available in arts and literature of the decade.

It is not always very profitable to study a decade as a period of time isolated from history, because time is a continuous process and its effect on history is to be traced all along at large. 1920s is an exception. The world changed at a rapid space towards the end of 19th century and results were felt intensely by the generation of thinkers and artists whose works appeared in 1920s. The seeds of change were sown as early as in the mid-19th century when the process of Industrial Revolution had set in. The labor pain began towards the end when Matthew Arnold confessed being caught in the "two worlds: one dead, other powerless to be born."[2] The baby was finally born as the new century dawned upon the world, and in 1920s it came of age. Charles Darwin, Karl Marx, Sigmund Freud, Sir James Frazer, and in America, Williams James, are among those who had fathered the baby, (please do not take the metaphor literally). The final stroke came from the First World War, which hastened the process of change at faster speed. G.S. Frazer's description of the effects of the war on England cannot be very different from its effects on the American society:

> The great war unsettled society in many ways. It has a great liberating effect; it hastened the emancipation of women; it promoted a temporary merging of social classes. Young men from humble background received commissions; young officers like Graves and Sassoon gained a new questioning attitude towards their inherited code. But above all, the First World War shattered Great Britain's rational self-confidence and produced doubts, uncertainty, and confusion. Instead of the thoughtless hopefulness of the Edwardian decade there was 'a new realism'—a tendency to think of man as a strictly limited creature. Man was no longer a giant figure striding to perfection, though he might achieve a certain decency through harsh self-discipline.[3]

The post-war decade experienced the social situation, which T.S. Eliot so effectively described as *The Wasteland* in Europe; in America group of young writers and artists were similarly judged by the matriarchal Gertrude Stein when she called them 'Lost Generation.'

The 'lost generation' experienced the traumatic experience of the war, the loss of religious faith, the rapid urbanization which shattered the old institution of family and marriage, the oncoming world of science which blew up the old myths and superstitions and the economic depression—all these produced a social situation which was no better than the wasteland. The young sensitive minds found it intolerable to exist, and, indeed, many of them decided not to. They killed themselves in order to escape the anguish they felt and the traumas they experienced. Those who survived often found themselves on the brink of madness. Hemingway offers an effective picture of his time in two collections of stories—*In Our Times* (1926) and *Men Without Women* (1926). Nick Adams, the Hemingway hero in the making grows up in an atmosphere, which is violent and hostile. He ends up as a spiritually broken adult finding it difficult to face the outer realities. Eugene O'Neil, another major modernist writer of the time, brings about the spiritual disillusionment in plays like *The Iceman Cometh, Morning Becomes Electra etc.*

T.S. Eliot's now famous poem *The Wasteland* is a true documentation of the social strain and degeneration, which pervaded during 1920s in both Europe and America.

Great art is born out of sufferings and the modernist art, great as it has been universally acknowledged, is no exception. Most of the modernist writers of 1920s as hinted earlier were on the brink of madness—but that madness, which Shakespeare placed closed to genius. Poets, lovers and lunatics were what constituted the "lost generation" the feeling of being 'lost' was the result of those socio-cultural factors which converted the entire west into the Wasteland. America had derived influences from Europe either through direct interaction or through the medium of intellectual awakening like debates, seminars, correspondence etc.

First World War created an independent chapter in the history of British poetry; in America, it produced prominent authors who wrote exclusively on war and its destructiveness. Ernest Hemingway is an example. Besides Hemingway, William Faulkner and John Dos Passos have written on war with deep concern and anguish. The wastefulness and destruction associated with war was a part of the wasteland that America was during 1920s.

The wasteland, however, proved to be a fertile soil for the literary spring. The decade's literary brilliance is displayed through these texts which were published during this single decade—*The Wasteland* (1922), the *Great Gatsby* (1925), *The Sun Also Rises* (1926), *The Sound and the Fury* (1929), *A Farewell to Arms* (1929), *The Bridge* (1929), *Tullips and Chimnery* (1923), *The American Tragedy* (1925), *Harmonium* (1923), etc. These titles are enough to suggest that America during 1920s was a socio-cultural Wasteland, but a literary spring.

Life magazine, in its issue of January 1950 described the twenties as a 'party' which everyone enjoyed—but a party that a nation cannot afford to have again, Frederick Hoffman continues the metaphor further, and calls it a party, which resulted in a serious hangover. According to him Americans still talk about a party but are repentant and resolved not to have it again. The 1920s were called "an age of wonderful nonsense," the time of "lost generation," the "jazz age," the "age of Freud, Zeigfield and Coolidge." This was the time of social hopelessness, of irresponsible young men and women who gave the nation the liveliest, freshest and the most stimulating writing in its literary experiences.

The decade, thus, was one of the most fruitful periods of the literary history of America. It produced remarkable writers of fiction like Hemingway, F. Fitzgerald, Katherene Ann Porter, Sherwood Anderson and William Faulkner-poets like Ezra Pound, Wallace Stevens, William Carlos Williams, E.E. Cumings, Carl Sandberg—and the playwright whose works remain unsurpassed till now—Eugene O'Neil. The literature these writers produced is mostly gloomy, for it was the producer of the wasteland, but as Shelley has put it one of the beautiful lyrics.

> We look before and after
> And pine for what is not,
> Our sincerest laughter
> With some pain is fraught,
> Our sincerest songs are those
> That tell of the saddest thought.[4]

Thus, the decade produced a literary spring through the social circumstances was gloomy and almost hopeless. The general mood of the literary creation is pessimistic and sad. The 19th century Naturalism with it's deterministic overtones loom large over the modernist writings of 1920s. This is demonstrated most effectively by Hemingway as a novelist.

As far as the novel of the decade is concerned, its achievement is equally remarkable. In choice of subject matter and settings, these writers moved in two different directions. Writers like

Faulkner, Katherene Ann Porter, Thomas Wolf, depicted the sad nostalgia for the South. A kind of regionalism emerged through the works of these novelists, which incorporates within itself a probing of cultural roots. They also deal with one of the major social issues America has faced since the civil war—the relation of the races and the status of the Negroes in America. Other writers like Hemingway and Fitzgerald write about the war and its aftermath. They draw upon their experiences of war and life in Europe, particularly in France. Their work tends to be cosmopolitan in nature and touch upon the various aspects of human existence in the traumatized social conditions of the 20th-century West.

Hemingway stands out among his contemporaries as a writer of immaculative style and substance. The following chapter is an attempt to demonstrate his concern as a novelist and their_relevance to our own times.

REFERENCES

1. Richard Hofstadler, *The Age of Reform: from Bryan to F.D.R.*. Jonathan Cape, 30 Bedford Square, London, 1962, pp. 23-59.
2. Mathew Arnold, *Grande Chartruse: Victorious Poetry: A Selection.* Macmillan (ed.), V.S. Seturaman, London, 1988, p. 142.
3. G.S. Fraser, *The Modern Writer and His World,* Penguin Books Ltd., Harmondsworth, Middlesex, 1970, pp. 96-97.
4. P.B. Shelley, Thomas Humphrey Ward (ed.), *The English Poet,* Macmillan, London, 1933, p. 386.

2

THE NOVELIST AND THE NOVELS—A BIOGRAPHICAL ACCOUNT OF HEMINGWAY AND IT'S IMPACT ON HIS WORK

> It is believed that a definitive biography of Hemingway will never be written, principally because no biographer can grasp the truth of his subject. Every assessment of Hemingway's life must therefore be at once a reassessment of his other 'lives' and the creation of new life—if for no other reason than, as Emerson puts it, that "every generation must write its own books."[1]

Ernest Hemingway, a multifaceted personality was born on July 21, 1899 at Oak Park, a suburb of Chicago, Illinois. He lived a legendary life and produced profound literature. His life and works were inter dependent. In fact, he turned his life experiences into a literature, which proved to be of great interest to readers. His writing made him a literary giant of twentieth century America, and won him Pulitzer Prize for fiction in 1953 and the Nobel Prize for literature in 1954.

Oak Park was considered as the capital of the middle class people of the world and was dominated by the Puritan values of the Victorian age. His father Dr. Clarence Edmond was a man devoted to outdoor activities like hunting, fishing etc. besides practicing medicine. His mother, Grace, was a woman with great interest in opera and piano. The Hemingway family believed in traditional values of the Puritan age; was devoutly religious and tried to impose their convictions and conventions upon their six children, two sons and four daughters. Ernest was the second child in the family.

It was against this background that Ernest Hemingway was brought up and educated. He declined to go for higher education. Instead he craved for actions and adventures and wanted to enrol himself in the American Army. But his damaged eye came in the way of his ambition and the Army rejected him. He, therefore, developed interest and skill in those sports where everything depends solely on one's own skill and where there was one to one confrontation, one antagonist is pitted against another like man against man; man against animal; man against fish; matador against bull etc. Mysteriously accident prone, as if secretly he wanted to expose himself to danger, Ernest Hemingway put to test his ability to absorb infliction.

Ernest Hemingway married four subsequent times. Before marriage, he had fallen in love with Agnes Von Kurowsky, an American Red Cross nurse who was elder to him by seven years. it was a cow and calf love. Ernest was disappointed when she turned down his offer of marriage. In September 1921, he met a young, rich, pianist; lady of St. Louis of Chicago named Hadley Richardson and married her. Ernest was very happy when Hadley accepted him and felt his love returned. Hadley too loved him very much but this could not last long. He divorced her when he was falling out of love with her. Ernest Hemingway met another young lady of St. Louis named Pauline Pfeiffer, a fashion designer, felt in her love and married her in the middle of 1927. She was Roman Catholic. Ernest Hemingway also became converted to Catholicism after the marriage.

On December 6, 1928 he received the news of the suicide of his father. He loved and admired his father in spite of the senior Hemingway's fluctuating nature. Naturally, this news inflicted incalculable adverse impact upon him. He not only grieved but also profoundly got disturbed by his father's lack of courage and his inability to face adversity unflaggingly. His father was considered as hen-pecked husband. He had collapsed under extreme pressure. Ernest Hemingway could not stop feeling himself that his father had failed in an essential aspect of living. He thought that he had not only failed but had somehow failed Ernest also. His father's failure was in a direct sense a challenge to him. The flaw in the father alerted the son more keenly than ever to feel concerned with his own moral and emotional strength.

Ernest Hemingway demanded the best in food, drink and comfort. His personal living expenses went up very high when he began making money from his best selling novels. His second marriage developed serious strain. He fell in love with Martha Gallhorn, his companion in Spain, newspaperwoman covering battlefront and a fiction writer. She had traveled widely as a foreign correspondent and had published excellent short stories. Ernest married her in 1940 after divorcing Pauline. This was his third marriage. Martha was an ambitious lady. Once Ernest fell ill and was hospitalized in Paris. He was attended upon by Mary Welsh, a beautiful lady who was also a newspaperwoman. She eventually becomes the fourth and the last wife of Ernest Hemingway, on March 14, 1946 as his marriage with Martha broke up in 1944. The fourth marriage lasted seventeen years and ended with Ernest's death. Unlike the other three marriages, this was his longest, happiest and most harmonious one.

Ernest Hemingway lived his life on his own terms and continued to write till death. He thought that a writer never retires from his writing. He always faced the question—what is he working on now? He died on July 2, 1961 by shooting himself through head when he could not bear pain and suffering of illness, high blood pressure and psychological difficulties that became oppressive at his fag-end of life and when things became rare to which he had lived and enjoyed. Thus, the colorful life of a great modernist writer in America came to the end.

Ernest Hemingway's writings are under scrutiny now from many angles. The feminists ask for judging his writings more carefully as they find his relations with women rather dubious. They want to consider Hemingway's work from the androgynous point of view. It is understood of him that he always advocated a masculine society. From 1921 to his death in 1961, he was consecutively married to four women without any significant pause between the marriages. He lived never without women in his life. From cradle to grave he did not free himself from the softening influence of woman.

Through training, discipline, death or other causes he depended upon women though he certainly did his best to think and write with enormous success, without women. He was raised androgynously by his parents.

Though he loved both to sew and to shoot his gun from childhood but he still loved his 'mama kitty.' He in fact was raised by the blend of both male and female version. While his father tried to raise him as the frontier scout, the mother impressed upon him naturalistic lore.

She named him as Ernest Miller Hemingway after the names of two Christian businessmen she most admired: her father Ernest and her Uncle Miller. His mother was searching her own image in Ernest. What she wanted for her son was very much for her own self. She twinned him with his older sister and began experimenting with their hairstyle, first Dutch length in infancy, than close cut. Ernest began to go to school and received his first boy's haircut. In such odd ways his mother used to express her own need to find a place for her considerable talent in a culture that encouraged man to pursue careers and encouraged woman to choose motherhood. Therefore, Ernest might have been under the influence of such desires wanted to do things in his adult years. Though Ernest Hemingway had quarreled lifelong against androgyny and always had drawn his masculine blow, he finally had been failure and resolved his quarrel with androgyny.[2]

Some of his luminous contemporaries were Ezra Pound, Sherwood Anderson, Gertrude Stein, F. Scott Fitzgerald, and others. He himself was a highly intelligent, widely read man of the time. He sought their help in writing but eventually the relationship with them became strained.

Hemingway writings reflect the undercurrents of the contemporary society followed by war. His massive experience with violence, war, sex, hunting, fishing etc. is reflected in his writing. He began to write when he was sixteen. He began his writing under the influence and encouragement of his English teacher Miss Dixon, for school weekly named *Trapeze*. He went to his uncle in Kansas City in search of a job and found one in the newspaper *Kansas City Star*, as a cub reporter.

This was one of the great newspapers in the country during that period. Thus, his career of writing begins. Hemingway produced 64 short stories and 16 vignettes. There were still more than three hundred books unpublished at the time of his death. He published his first short story 'Judgement of Manitou' in 1916. It was an imitation of Ring Lardner. He accepted the editorship of *Cooperative Commonwealth* a journal of the cooperative societies of the United States of America in 1920. He published his *Three Stories and Ten Poems* in 1923 which contained 'Up in Michigan,' 'Out of Season,' and 'My Old Man'. He began to make attempt at writing poems but soon he realized that his talent does not lie in poetry. He concentrated on fiction. In 1924 he published *in our time,* a collection of miniature of 32 pages from Paris. Later, 'Boni And Liveright' published in book form along with 14 short stories under the title *In Our Time*.

At 18, he was exposed to life and death of most savage form and had a taste of illness and pain while accompanying his father on medical calls. At Kansas City he witnessed full range of human misery from the distorted lives of criminals to the shattered bodies of hospital inmates. He was also exposed to habits and attitudes of newspaper reporters in whom he found outer shell of cynicism and toughness and inwardly often tender and sentimental. Therefore, he had adopted the combination of toughness and tenderness in his writings.

In the spring of 1918, Hemingway left the *Star* and joined the Red Cross. He was then sent to the Italian front where his first assignment was to distribute Red Cross packages of chocolates to the Italian soldiers in the trenches. There he witnessed the horrible scenes of mortar shell explosion. An Austrian mortar shell exploded squarely in the trench, which killed instantly one Italian soldier on one side and another fell on the ground the other side, both legs of whom were badly shattered. Hemingway, who was standing thereby, received injuries. Dozens of fragments of shell entered into his left leg. He fainted from shock. When he regained consciousness it seemed to him that his soul, like a handkerchief blown away by a sudden gust of wind, had left body and that at the last moment he had reached out and pulled back.

When war ended, Ernest Hemingway found himself unfit to live ordinary civil life at home. He took up writing and wrote poems and short stories, which no publisher was prepared to accept. His parents too were not happy about his writings and regarded his writing as pointless and wastage. Hemingway then went to Toronto in early 1920 in search of a job. There he got a job of a reporter for the *Toronto Star Weekly,* where he got encouraged to dig up events and write features of general interest. He was also given a chance to express his sense of humor and irony. But he left this job and returned home. At home he left idle. This annoyed his mother and a bitter quarrel developed. The quarrel had chastening effect upon Hemingway. He then got a job in Chicago of writing advertising copy, for a real estate firm. But this did not inspire him. He began to write again, producing sketches, anecdotes, short stories etc., chiefly about events in Europe during war.

Ernest Hemingway was gravitating into the literary circle when Chicago became the hub of writers. He met Sherwood Anderson who found in Ernest willingness and enthusiastic pupil. Later, Anderson sent him to Paris, a city of young writers and artists. Paris was intellectually alive then. Hemingway was introduced to Gertrude Stein who was living in Paris. He quit the advertisement job and resumed his earlier connections with *Star Weekly* believing that of all occupations reporting was probably closest to creative writing.

In December 1921 he accepted a post of foreign correspondent offered by a sister newspaper named *Daily Star* and this gave him an opportunity to cover various political conferences in Germany, Italy, Near East and interviewed large number of people. He covered the bloody conflict of 1922 between Turkey and Greece, which was painfully tragic for him.

The hard work of writing started bearing fruits and six of his poems were published in January 1923 issue of Harriet Monroe's Magazine *Poetry*. In the summer of 1923 Robert Mc Almon, Ernest's friend brought out a 300-copy edition of Hemingway's first book called *Three Stories And Ten Poems*. In January 1924 his another friend William Bird, owner of the Tree Mountains Press in Paris published 170 copies of a second small book *In Our Time,* containing sketches drawn from Hemingway experiences of World War-I and the Greco-Turkish war including Spanish bullfighting. Sherwood Anderson was immensely pleased with him and urged his New York publishers Boni and Liveright to bring out a volume of Hemingway's stories to which they yielded and as a result the first American edition of *In Our Time* appeared in his own country in October 1925. This contained all sketches of the Bird edition, two of the three stories of McAlmon and ten new stories. F. Fitzgerald, like Anderson, came forward to help Hemingway. This book also contains the Hemingway stories of Nick Adams who was to pioneer the Hemingway hero, a typical masculine character who is the protagonist of all major Hemingway fiction.

The title *In Our Time* is taken from the *Book of Common Prayer*: *Give Me Peace In Our Time, O Lord*. Ironically, Hemingway's writings offer little peace, Nick Adams, a small boy, is initiated into the world of violence, pain and death as he matures through different stages. In the 'Indian Camp' Nick with his doctor-father sees an American Indian committing suicide by cutting his throat with a razor because he cannot bear the pain of his wife, who undergoes a caesarian delivery by a doctor with a pocketknife. There is hardly any doubt that Nick and his father, Dr. Adams are modeled after Ernest and Dr. Hemingway. In fact, the stories here are not the stories of Nick Adams because he is only an observer watching and learning besides noticing the pain, violence and evil in the world. His experiences are the experiences of his generation. He experiences a gradual disillusionment with the other sex both in his mother and in his girlfriend. He drinks, is wounded, and makes a separate peace with the enemy. The wound he gets is both physical and psychological. It is fishing that gives him a relief from the above affliction. The Hemingway hero confronts overpowering universe, sustains irreversible catastrophe and achieves transcendence. The Hemingway hero chooses this path, challenges the cosmos, confronts and sustains tragedy but wins with dignity and ascertains the self. The hero sacrifices his life but takes away the larger victory. Hemingway believes that all great novels are tragedies because greatness emanating from dignity and grandeur refuses to give in to the worldly forces.

Charles Darwin's book *The Origin of Species* (1859) set down the trends, which changed the entire thinking of man about himself and of the universe. Darwin's theory of evolution and the concept of "survival of the fittest," formulated a new theory. According to this theory, man's fate at the moment of his birth is determined by the outer factors. They could be social, economic, or even biological. Man is a helpless creature, fighting a lonely battle against these ferociously hostile forces. The rise of naturalistic novel towards the end of nineteenth century is often attributed to this concept of man and the universe. Hemingway owes his notion of man and the universe to Naturalism in American fiction of which Hemingway is a powerful exponent.

Hemingway adopted the Darwinian theory called determinism. To him man is born to lose for one reason or another. He is fated to do so in an unequal battle with the hostile forces in the universe or because he carries something inherently that brings the universe crashing down upon him. The man loses the battle in flesh and spirit to possess nobility, grandeur and heroism. Determinism in fact, was the guiding principle to almost all the modernist writers in America. Hemingway is thus a representative of his generation who lived and wrote during 1920s.

Hemingway developed a style of writing, longer, complex and artistic fiction. He wrote novels on the new trends prevalent in American society in twentieth century. His novels represent new events and their result on the individual characters. Hemingway captured imagination of American people. The nineteenth-century American fiction concerned itself vague issues like human values including sympathy towards the blacks. Hemingway's concern was different, because he obviously lived in different conditions, which prevailed in America in the early decades of twentieth century. He chose to write about negative values of the American life and society, as these values were strongly felt and experienced by thinking minds of the day.

As it happens, the protagonist in Hemingway's novel is ultimately defeated. However, the defeat of man Hemingway portrays in his novels is the outward defeat. He believes that the outward defeat is for the sake of inward victory. Writ William quotes Robert Carringan saying:

> Man's tragic condition is that he is doomed by faith to defeat. It is impossible to win except through total defeat and even destruction. Such a victory is itself transcendental.[3]

America is a kind of paradise of domestic security and wealth. Technical advancements have provided comforts. The early twentieth-century American society was full of complexities. An American set an example to the world of a new man and of a new order. The Americans were about to risk their future on a new experimental way during this period. They believed that violence will not rule the world in the long run. Therefore, the United States of America must defend its safety and success and believed that war and preparation for war are blunders; every dollar invested in industry is a means of overthrowing their enemy more effectively than a thousand dollar spent on frigates or standing armies. The American success lies in economy, not in war. However, this belief gave rise to confusion among the American intellectuals, which led to contradictions and rapacity.

Every American seemed to have nourished the idea that he is doing whatever he could, to overthrow tyranny which the past had imposed upon their minds. He believed in what Jefferson had pointed out, namely, that man would improve morally with their physical and intellectual growth.

Hemingway exactly perceives this subtle nature of American society and depicts it in his novels. Twentieth-century American literature refused to adopt Mark Twain's sympathy for Negroes as in *Huckleberry Finn,* and Hemingway is the prime example. He on the other hand, shared the Negro experience and gets involved in his sense of morality. He is not a detached observer of brutality as it occurs to men (the Negroes included), but the one who is a part of the whole experience.

He agrees with the view that all American writings spring from *Huckleberry Finn,* but also realizes that Twain's humanity and morality end with the arrival of the modern world. Human elements disappear from Hemingway's writings cautiously and knowingly. It is so because Hemingway has witnessed cruel factors operating in the human society, which became important ingredients of his fiction.

War, violence, love and sex are the major factors on which Hemingway works. He had himself participated in the First World War in which he was severally wounded. He also had sexual relations with woman, which had a great impact upon his creative sensibility. He had thought of war as a romantic enterprise, where one would put to test his personal courage and heroism. But his experience in the war led him to disillusionment as he discovered that in modern warfare the scope for individual heroism does not exist and he himself was not been able to do anything heroic. This made him create and develop in his writing a hero who was imaginary extension of his own self, a fictitious man. Hemingway wished that the readers should read his fiction as an extended autobiography.

The Torrents of Spring appeared in the spring of 1926. The title has been taken from Ivan Turgenev's book entitled *The Torrents of Spring* written in 1870. He wrote it in a single week. This was a short, blistering title parody, part novel, part sketch, part spoof, ridiculing Sherwood Anderson's *Dark Laughter.* This short piece of writing was both a climax and a turning point in Hemingway's relationship with his literary comrades. This piece of literature ridiculed and parodied Anderson's style of writing, his characters and his most cherished ideas about life. As a result, Hemingway's friendship with Anderson came to an end. This book, of course, did not sell well but it revealed Hemingway's writing potentials. It contained the art of parody, satire, wit and humor.

During the interval between the first and second marriages Hemingway lived alone in Paris and continued to write short stories, which were published in 1926 under the title *Men Without Women*. This included among other famous stories 'The Killers,' 'Fifty Grand,' 'In Another Country,' and 'The Undefeated.' These stories deal with the subjects like gangsters, prizefighters, soldiers and bullfighters.

At about the same time *The Sun Also Rises* appeared. That was in October 1926. It was a fiction of frustrated men and women subsidized for carousing, poor in psychic resources who drift about and drink in Paris and Spain. The protagonist of the novel Jake Barnes is shot through in the First World War. His penis was damaged but not the testicles, and hence he could possess normal sex urge but was incapable of consummation. Once he surveyed his damaged part in the mirror beside his bed and cried himself to sleep. Brett Ashley, a modern American woman overflowing with sexual urge though sleeps with several men like Cohn, Michel Campbell and Pedro Romero, loves Jake Barnes with whom normal sex was impossible. Both, Brett and Jake try to live together but only to mutual frustration. Jake, thus disillusioned by the war, tries to find new values in life, becomes aficionado-passionate about bullfighting—but finds incapable of sexual intercourse, still trying to face life with courage, endurance and dignity. Brett is also no fertility goddess.

She is the Wasteland to use T.S. Eliot's imagery. All expatriates in the novel are derelicted-uprooted from home, country and former values, by the war and its aftermath. They no longer depend on outmoded code like romanticism or on organized religion to solve their problems. This was a common dilemma faced by the modernist writers in America, whom Gertrude Stain has described as the *Lost Generation*.

Thus, the emphasis shifted from courage to the efficiency of the machine in which romantic notion of man: brave, virile, sporting, hardworking, a kind of Macho figure, individual courage and heroism, finds no place. It is a senseless war. Man does not have to rely on his own inner resources but on sophisticated weapons. The only courageous thing to do is to walkout of it. Thus, Hemingway effectively brings out futility and destructiveness of war.

A Farewell to Arms, another of his beautiful novels came out in 1929. It was considered as *Romeo and Juliet* of Ernest Hemingway. It is a love story set against a sharply realistic background of fighting in the war and the tension arising in northern Italy. The story centers around an American volunteer painting peculiar pathos of young love flowering in a hostile universe. The novel offers remarkable description of war on the Italian front. It is superbly fused with the private lives of the hero and the heroine.

A Farewell to Arms combines the two themes—those of love and war—effectively together. It also presets symbolically the quest for alternate God, replacing the one who is said to be dead. Henry belongs to the 'lost generation' who is bored with life surrounded by war and its futility. Therefore, love for him assumes the form of God, to which he must dedicate totally. He deserts war, makes a separate peace with himself, and joins his beloved away from the fronts of war. In the meantime, Catherine becomes pregnant and the life for the lovers becomes horrible. Henry charged of cowardice and infidelity to the nation, is being chased by the police. The lovers row across the lake and reach Switzerland, where the situation is less hostile and where the police will not be able to get hold of him. But he worse awaits in Switzerland. Exhausted by the overnight journey by lake, Catherine develops pain and labor. She is hospitalized where the medical facilities are meager, far from being adequate. Consequently she dies in childbirth following an unsuccessful caesarian. Henry is left alone. He has already lost reputation of a brave lieutenant as he has deserted war when it was actually being fought, now he has lost love for which he has willingly accepted humiliation.

Thus, the novel ends in gloom and sadness. Hemingway is highly successful in his attempt to associate the readers mind with war, death, pain, sadness and gloom.

Love for woman to Hemingway is the one-way traffic. It is one-sided relationship. He does not believe in 'give and take' relationship. Henry has no intention whatsoever of loving Catherine. But Catherine loves Henry with devotion. This makes Henry to fall in her love. Eventually, Catherine becomes pregnant and falls in the biological trap.

> The separate peace declared by Frederic Henry was a tactic which carried the full force of the author's own commitment. Neither the author nor the character could as easily evade the implications of the 'biological trap,' one could always detect the tuneless outline of nature-not a romantic resource expressing beauty and truth but a constant comment on man's insignificance.[4]

Catherine dies of childbirth. The child is also stillborn. Henry is left alone in the wide world. Thus, the novel epitomizes the whole of the American response to the First World War. It thus, becomes a representative of its time.

The esthetic success of the novel brought Hemingway to the height of the fame and freed him from poverty he was facing for long. By this time Hemingway had developed certain prickliness about the intellectuals. He began to scorn professionals and academic critics. His friends who were writers in the twenties were replaced by the non-literary persons, sailors, sportsman and unclassified free-lance figures in thirties. Hemingway though himself was highly intellectual and widely read, believed that there is "no pleasure in anything if you mouth it up too much."[5]

Death in the Afternoon is a non-fiction. It was published in 1932. it describes bullfighting in Spain. It depicts the fighting and ethics of bullring. Hemingway paints vividly the horror and danger to which the bullfighter is constantly exposed. He believes that death is the ultimate reality and that the man realizes his potentiality only on the face of the death. Hemingway saw in the bullfighting a modern hero who could give meaning to his existence by the manner he faces danger continually.

Hemingway makes a tragedy rather than a crude slaughter. He gives minute description of each stage of the bullfight and of the whole theory of the slow wearing down of the bull by picadors and banderillas, so that, in the end the powerful animal now trimmed down in strength and the matador can meet on equal terms. The book offers a bitter comment on individual matador, his styles, habit and degree of courage; and extensive glossary of bullfight terms.

Green Hills of Africa was published in 1935. It was originally titled as *The Highlands of Africa* but it was discarded in favor of *Green Hills of Africa*. Hemingway described his own exciting experiences of African safari. It mainly deals with hunting adventures. The book has prose, which sings like poetry without ever ceasing to be prose. It is easy, intricate and magical. Hemingway lifts up the whole place of African hills and places them into the mind of reader and the reader finds hills, plains, natives, animals, rivers and trees before his eyes. The novel successfully communicates the sense of the place; one can see, smell, taste, feel and hear these things with the author.

Green Hills of Africa compares the life of a writer with that of the hunter and a meaningful relationship of man with nature is brought out. Hemingway observed that the civilized man, particularly of the West, has alienated himself from nature but the man from Africa lives in very close touch with it. This was a new inspiration for Hemingway, which he carried lifelong.

To Have and Have Not a novel published in 1937 is about the personal life of one freelance fishing boat operator, who was unable to earn his living by legitimate means because of great economic depression America. Harry Morgan, a fishing boat operator, is a 'have-not' but he has other different qualities like self-reliance, honesty, toughness, sexual vigor, courage and uncompromising nature, which Hemingway regards as very important and essential for man. Hemingway, through Harry Morgan, tries to convey that these qualities are the wealth for human being. A man economically poor can be rich in other aspects such as these qualities. Harry Morgan though lost his one arm in the shooting that ensued in smuggling, it did not make him incapable to fight against the world. He even asserts himself at the end. For this he suffers stoically and heroically. He believed that "a man alone has no chance in the world."[6]

This novel arouses consciousness and the belief that man must live within the ethics provided by the society, in order to improve his own life and that of the poor lot. It is a satire on the plight of an unemployed man.

For Whom the Bell Tolls is most ambitious novel of Ernest Hemingway. It was published in 1940. The title of the novel was taken from Donne's *Meditation No. 17*. The title suggests the inevitability of the human predicament from which there is no escape. It is a novel about the Spanish Civil War and the struggle for the Spanish people against fascism. Thus, it can be considered as the novel of fate of a Republic and it's people who are caught in the Civil War.

The fatal wound of the hero in *For Whom the Bell Tolls,* American named Jordan and the title of the novel, convey a pessimistic sense that for every one death lurks around the corner; the funeral bell that tolls for others may toll for you as well. "Philip Young points out that this novel deals with psychological and autobiographical aspects."[7] Jordan, the hero of the novel is semi-autobiographical hero like Nick Adams and Frederic Henry. He succeeds in the mission of blowing bridge to check the advancement of the fascists. He is fatally wounded and suffers stoically but does not leave the place of his position. He gives the message that "if we win here we will win everywhere. The world is fine place and worth fighting for and I hate very much to leave" (193). This remark is perhaps addressed to the cowardly act of suicide committed by Ernest Hemingway's father who could not face the situation in the family and who, finally, succumbed to death.

Hemingway tries to convey that the physical wound may heal but not the psychic wound. The psychic wound remains painful. Love-making can heal the psychic wound. This proves true in the case of Maria, the heroine of the novel, who was raped by the fascist earlier. This has inflicted upon her the psychic wound. This wound remains painful to her. However, intense lovemaking with Jordan gives her relief. The author has no intention to create room for erotic relationship. His sole purpose is expose the psychological wound and to suggest the cure. Maria is a typical woman in the modernist writings in both Europe and America. She is submissive to the man and demands nothing in return. She is typical of the Hemingway woman who is a prototype of the modernist concept of man woman relationship. Unlike other novels, this novel was not welcomed in Russia because of the author's vague ideology. The Russians had expected something different. Jordan does not conform to the communist concept of class factors and works out his plans according to his own designs.

Across the River and Into the Trees was published in September 1950 with great hopes of best selling but was a commercial failure. However, as the time passed, the novel was considered a classic and Hemingway was compared with Shakespeare. Later, the sell of the book improved.

Across the River and Into the Trees is a symbolic study of a complex state of mind. The title of the novel is borrowed from the last words of General Stonewall Jackson who fought in the American civil War. His last words were 'Let us cross the river and rest under the shed of trees.' The protagonist of the novel Richard Cantwell is a retired colonel. He goes to Venice for duck shooting where he falls in love with Renata, nineteen year old Italian countess. The name Renata was borrowed by Hemingway from Renata Borgetti whom Hemingway had met in 1923. She is the idealized girl closer to Hawthorne heroines than to Catherine or Maria. Cantwell shares some of the qualities of Hemingway. He is strong, stoic and professional soldier. Like Hemingway he was wounded, carried the scar and could not forget the past. The colonel feels himself an old man and calls Renata his daughter. Hemingway too had began calling himself 'Papa' when he found himself old after his father's death and to Andriana Ivancich (lover), daughter. But Renata is not Andriana Ivancich.

Colonel Cantwell appears as war-scarred, embittered professional soldier against the backdrop of love and death.

Renata appears to be animated doll having no demands or expectations of her own. Colonel Cantwell seemed to take more interest in activities other than war. He loves his young beloved and takes to drinks.

Hemingway's acclaimed novel *The Old Man and the Sea* appeared in 1952. Russia too received it well and with enthusiasm. Vladislov Droby Shevski considered it a tragedy of a poor fisherman in the capitalist world in which he will not submit to the dollar and will not lower his head before the cannon's mouth. While in Cuba in April 1932, Hemingway had discovered the art of fishing under the guidance of Carlos Gutierrez who was later named as Santiago, as the protagonist of the novel. The novel depicts Santiago as poor, unlucky, old, Cuban fisherman. After getting nothing for 84 days he, on eighty-fourth day catches a big marlin only to lose it to voracious sharks. He struggles single-handedly against the sharks but succeeds only in bringing in skeleton of the fish leftover. During the struggle he fights, prays,. invokes the courage of his youth. Though he loses in the end he does not consider himself 'defeated.' Hemingway conveys through Santiago that 'a man can be destroyed but not defeated.'

The novel is considered as a masterpiece of modern American writings. Hemingway elevated a simple fisherman to the rank of a hero. The struggle of Santiago draws considerably the appreciation and sympathy of readers for his valor, courage, persistent struggle and humility. The loneliness, hunger, sleep, tiresomeness, lack of effective weapons etc cannot extinguish his courage. He prays God not because he is weak and invokes support but as a man he pleads his cause with dignity. The old man maintains tranquil and placid state of mind throughout his struggle.

The novel symbolizes many things to many people. Hemingway has conveyed a plurality of meanings to the human society. According to him it is a struggle of the whole humanity against the cruel forces of the world. It is a struggle of an artist against his unsympathetic critics and reviewers. Santiago with wounded hands in the struggle brings himself close to Jesus Christ. The old man in the struggle remembers Manolo, his fishing companion who is a young boy. Manolo is to Santiago what youth is to age; pupil to the teacher and son to the father. Hemingway gives the message to the human society that even though there is uneven might and devastation of machine man can assert himself; can refuse to be beaten and defeated. The world is exclusively of man. This novel won him Pulitzer Prize for fiction in 1953 and also the Nobel Prize for literature in 1954.

Island in the Stream was published posthumously in 1970 by his wife Mary Hemingway with the help of his publishers Philip Young and Charles Scribner. Originally, it was titled as *The Island and the Stream* and was written ten years before his death. Mary Hemingway made some modification in the original script of the book before its final publication.

The novel deals with the life of an American painter named Thomas Hudson and his family. He has Hemingway's resemblance in personality. Both Hudson and Hemingway have common features; both are artists, sensitive and have problem with their marriages; they divorce their wives, their sons die. Hemingway's two sons Patric and Gregory died in car accident in 1947. This is obvious in this novel in the death of Andrew and David, the two sons of Hudson, in automobile accident. Hudson's third son is killed by Nazi anti-aircraft gun. These three sons had come to Hudson to fill the void in the life of their father during holidays. Hudson lives on the boat—the only house he has on the backdrop of the vast ocean. It was his petrol boat called 'Q Boat' and is based on Hemingway's experiences on the boat 'Pilar' in 1942. Hudson dies finally in the chase of a Nazi submarine. In fact, Hudson is surrounded by death all the times. The large looming presence of death is the Hemingway's own environment which is common to most of his novels.

The dominant image in the novel is that of Infinite Ocean. The Gulf Stream is connected with the universe, the infinite cosmos, which manifest creation and the principal of life in it. Set in the background of sea is the house of Thomas Hudson, the image of temporary shelter for rest and peace. Certain inscrutability is associated with the sea; it permits a happy and exciting occasion for under-water fishing and then sends sharks to destroy the joy bringing imminent fear of death. Nature is not always cooperative to the design of man. Nature and sea are the cradle and the grave of man there is no escape from them. But unmindful of the consequences, Hemingway has great faith in man's power of tolerance and bravery in the face of odds of life. Most of his characters, as Hudson in this novel, project Hemingway's faith in man's tendency and endurance.

The Garden of Eden was posthumously published by a talented editor Tom Jenks in readable form in 1986, twenty-five years after the author's death. Reviewers say that the Hemingway writings continue to influence present writers. The novel focuses on disintegrated marriage and the crisis in the personal life and career of a successful young writer, David, one of the most sophisticated heroes of Hemingway fictions. He is World War I veteran and the acclaimed author. His wife Catherine is also a writer. Their mutual devotion to and delight in each other at first seem complete and idealistic. This was indeed the Garden of Eden in biblical terms. David is obviously Hemingway's autobiographical hero. But soon enough this Garden of Eden reveals the presence of snake. Catherine transforms herself physically and psychologically. She cuts her hair short like a boy's and begins playing teasing games that hint exchange of_sexual identities. She initiates a friendship with David, an attractive young woman, Marita, and entices David into an amorous sharing of their lives. Troubled and guilty, David retreats into writing of along story about elephant hunting in Africa relying on his childhood memories of elephant hunting with his father in Africa.

Catherine's jealousy of David's work precipitates a crisis. The situation develops somewhat similar to the time Hemingway and his first wife Hadley spent a summer, living with Pauline Pfeiffer. Catherine is a spoiler whose taste is a forbidden fruit, who threatens the private Eden of David's art. David and Catherine Bourne spent much time in drinking. David was aware of the potential damage alcohol does to a writer but he is tender and vulnerable and is unable to avoid the situation.

The story is a sort of a ritual adolescent tale of imitation into the ferocity of the grown up and echoes disillusionment and betrayal. Hemingway's heartfelt sense of women as a source of evil enforces and energies the allegory. Catherine is transformed from sexually docile Eve into caustic and destructive bitch. Hemingway has depicted her as an evil for the failure of spouses. The story had contemporary relevance adding up to the feminist debate on man-woman relationship.

In the course of the novel Catherine realizes her inadequacy of the employment of language and cannot write. She blames that literature is male controlled. She therefore turns to alternative medium of expression—her own body creates text, not with language but with her body, insisting on a transsexual relationship with her husband. She expects David to act as a scribe *i.e.,* she wants to transfer to paper or to translate into language the story that she wants to create. She provides the plot by living it moment by moment. She herself cannot write and develops a belief that phallocentric control of letters produced similar effects on the female writer. She also believes that the female libido and not the written word best expresses reality. David calls her "Devil" for her seemingly unacceptable attitude.

Thus, Catherine rebels actively. She bleaches her hair, entices David to change his coiffure, engages in transsexual and bisexual relations. She desires both self respect and sexual satisfaction from communicating with her body, visits local café and tells David that "stupid people will think it's strange." She expects complete sexual gratification or *jouissance*. She speaks libidinal language. However, with all this she never feels she had full access to or command over traditional phallocentric state and gets frustration.

Patriarchal control of literature has profoundly crippled female psyche. Highly creative women suffer from mental disease or diseases like agoraphobia, anorexia and claustrophobia. Garden of Eden reflects anxiety of authorship felt by woman and radical fear that she can never become a "Precursor" and that the act of writing will isolate or destroy her. They develop a belief that if they do not behave like angels, they must be monsters.

David rejects what Catherine wants him to do. He insists that Catherine should play the role of domesticity, passive, and submissive wife. David creates the inevitable opposition between the two.

The novel also offers contrast between Catherine and Marita's attitude towards money. Women have unrestricted and unlimited tendency towards spending, dispense gifts freely, fearing no loss or embarrasses. Marita practices this sort of female economy. Catherine follows this and wants to support David financially. David manifests male economy where money is commodity to be possessed, which signifies power and sexual control. He equates Catherine's financial support with loss of psychosexual dominance and tries to be free of such debt.

As a result, she openly and vehemently criticizes not only David's character but his writing ability as well. Finally, she discovers herself from the bond of her relationship with David and Marita and destroys David's manuscripts in a final effort to ensure work on her own narrative. She leaves Paris for the illustration and publication of her book. She defies social and sexual taboos and initiates new parameters for relationships.

Thus, Catherine symbolizes larger potential revolution, which will result from woman's liberation. Catherine's firm belief that her libido will produce far more radical effects of political and personal change, that some might like to think about a mutation in human relations, in all praxis. This thinking will substantially alter social, potential and sexual codes. Hemingway provides human society to see beyond restrictive binaries *i.e.* male-female, homosexuality-heterosexuality, passive-active and wants to enrich an understanding between man and man.[8]

Short Stories

There are two collections of short stories attribute to Hemingway. *In Our Time* (1925), and *Men Without Women* (1926). Critics have pointed out that Hemingway is better short story writer than novelist. It may not be completely true but there are indeed well known and best short stories written by him. Among them are: 'The Killers,' 'A Clean Well Lighted Place,' 'The Short Happy Life of Francis Macomber,' 'Old Man at the Bridge,' 'Fifty Grand,' 'The Snows of Kilimanjaro,' 'Hills Like White Elephants,' 'Big Two Hearted River,' 'Soldiers' Home,' etc. Most of the stories describe man's alienation from himself and from society. They either deal with war, violence or death and man's reaction to the crisis. Hemingway projects through these stories courage, endurance and zeal.

In Hemingway's works we can recognize the right of sacrifice, the right sexual union, the right of conversion and of the symbolic death and rebirth. However, Hemingway does not believe in the presence of these rights in society unnecessarily. Hemingway world abounds in primitivism and the rituals associated with it, which has a source of inspiration to great art_and is explicitly present in the works of great modernist. Hemingway firmly believes that there is nothing to be ashamed of to be guilty about primitivism, because it presents man in his total naturalness and in uncorrupt form, away from the so-called civilization. Hemingway inaugurates a new genre unknown hitherto to the readers of American fiction. Hemingway, not through his identification with guilty acts of Oedipus and Macbeth or a media by suffering their passionate shoulders, but by being gored with a bull, hooked with a fish, impaled with a grasshopper on a fishhook, not by identifying himself with human heroes, but by those who are indeed defeated.

On the social level the writing of Hemingway performs a function similar to that of the stereotype. It conditions the readers to accept the less worthy values of society and it serves to justify and absolve our sins of social irresponsibility. With unconscious irony Hemingway fiction advises stoic acceptance of those conditions of life which it so accurately describes and which it so presents to reject. Thus, Hemingway fiction depictes individuals as not the masters of their fate but rather as without control over their destiny. Right does not always triumph, wickedness is not always punished, God is not in his heaven and all is not well with the world. Thus, the ideology of the modernism, which becomes a favorable theme of most of the American writers during the first two decades of this century, becomes obvious through Hemingway's fiction. Hemingway remains to this day a prominent exponent of American modernism.

REFERENCES

1. Quoted from Frank, Scafella (ed.), *Hemingway: Essays of Reassessment,* Oxford University Press, 1991, p. 9.
2. *Ibid.*, pp. 2-10.
3. Wirt Williams, *The Tragic Filed and Ernest Hemingway,* Louisiana State University Press, Balon Rouge and London, p. 1.
4. French Warren, *The Twenties,* 1922, p. 211.
5. Gurko Leo, *Ernest Hemingway and the Pursuit of Heroism,* Craw Well, New York, 1968, p. 39.
6. *Ibid.*, p. 41.
7. Rameshkumar Srivastava, *Hemingway and his For Whom the Bell Tolls,* Guru Nanak Dev University, Amritsar, 1980, p. 18.
8. Kathy Willingham, *Hemingway's The Garden of Eden, Writing with the Body, The Hemingway Review,* Vol. 12, No. 2, Spring, 1993, p. 60.

3

LOVE AND LABOR—THEMATIC ANALYSIS OF THE TEXTS

Hemingway is a true representative of his time in a sense that his novels offer a graphic account of the outer realities. He writes mainly about war, which was the haunting reality during the early decades of 20th century. He is concerned as a novelist with the sufferings men and women experienced during the war times. The war has created an independent chapter in the history of British poetry; in America it produced a writer like Hemingway who single-handedly demonstrated the futility and destructiveness of war. He is an artist who could see the intricacies of human relations in hard times and projected them through his hard work. These intricacies of the human relations offered him enormous scope to explore the human personality placed against the hostile circumstances created by the war. Thus, Hemingway's artistic vision encompasses within itself a total man who struggles with the outer odds, one who celebrates the victorious moments, does not give in easily to hostile circumstances, and then accepts his final defeat in recognition of his inability and helplessness before the omnipotent outer universe.

Hemingway has presented a fiction that could communicate the experiences with new meanings. His novels are for the redemption of modern man who is trapped in material values and suffers from *Nada:* the state of nothingness. In fact, Hemingway was searching for the happiness of common man in the public life and in the life of an individual. Public life includes duties and responsibilities, which make man's life meaningful. But to his utter dismay in both the public as well as in private life Hemingway observed that there is no happiness because man has become too self-centered and materialistic. The only solution in this predicament he observes is to survive. He observes that this world of ours is the irrelevant world. Survival in this irrelevant world is to have a sense of detachment and love life in maximum possible way. Whatever the time span available to life one must enjoy. Sometimes the life lies in the service of society and community and some times in the individual self. He has also expressed political views through his novels. However, he has no commitment to any particular political view or ideology. Sometimes, he favors communism, sometimes he criticizes it. He did not always favor capitalism but his love for democracy is explicit through his work. With all his writings Hemingway seems to have concluded that the rich people make war and the innocent common people suffer. Common man therefore must build up courage to fight for his survival and not to get frustrated. Though man has no control over his destinations as it is controlled by certain determining forces he must fight against them though to be defeated in the end. Hence. Hemingway's chief concern is to guard mankind against the evil factors, which surround him. He tries to eliminate those factors, which spoil man's endeavor for the dignity of life.

This chapter is intended to analyze the major novels of Hemingway and to explore his multidimensional views on man and the universe. Here is an attempt to comprehend these views in a way that would explain Hemingway's concept of love and labor, which ultimately lead to the human tragedy.

Ranging from accidental and individual suffering, Hemingway portrays the suffering of the collective mass, which is national and also international. He has depicted suffering of First World War in *A Farewell to Arms,* suffering of Spanish Civil War in *For Whom the Bell Tolls,* the suffering of the Second World War in the *Across the River and Into the Trees,* and in the *Island in the Stream.* Hemingway's fiction contains a large variety of human suffering—physical as well as psychological, both individual as well as collective. Suffering is depicted in various manifestations and they occur in the human context and also in the context of non-human beings.

Though Hemingway deals largely with war, his quest for peace continues. He hates violence. To him war is stupidity and misuse of the government machinery and power. Although war appears as a major theme in his writings Hemingway experiences his special sympathy for those who are the victims of war. For him war is not solution to the political or social problems. The present nuclear race is suicidal because with nuclear weapon war neither can be won nor lost. It is, therefore, necessary to avoid wars. Hemingway's novels are, therefore, relevant to the modern time, particularly to the developing countries and to the developing societies like India. The recent Indian nuclear explosion in which India takes pride will aggravate the suffering of Indian people rather than act as the security and protection.

Hemingway had seen the suffering from very close quarters, His personal life was full of suffering. He could also see the suffering of the people of underworld closely, when he worked on the road hopping freight, washing dishes in cheap cafes, working on docks and boxing for living.

America of 20's was abruptly thrown into the whirlpool of perils and in crisis, which was followed, by the great economic depression and Spanish Civil War. They brought to America the untold suffering of innumerable types. Hemingway's novels depict these sufferings realistically. These sufferings are sometimes physical, which may be accidental. They also are psychological sufferings like fear, anguish, anxiety, against-nada of man about his position in alien and indifferent universe. Hemingway reveals the physical suffering of people like prizefighter, bull fighter, gambler, peasant and priest. These are the simple set of people who suffer bravely till the last, though they hate the cause of their suffering. There is another set of people who are subjected to suffering, namely, the people who have the capacity to sustain, to make serious commitment in life and to the values. Such people have the capacity to stand up to face the alien universe. Their commitment carries them through the suffering.

Hemingway, has depicted in his writing the plight of individual in a world dominated by violence-human or technological. He also reveals the emotional strain and suffering his characters undergo. The psychologically wounded man may recover partially but a man suffered from the emotional shock stands no chance of recovery. Man can be emotionally hurt, anywhere, anytime, at any stage in life. There is no solution for the recovery of such man except suicide. This emotional suffering is very well exposed in the short story, *The Clean Well Lighted Place,* which depicts the trauma of war and its devastating effects or the human psyche.

Hemingway's failure in love for nurse Agnes produced deep impact on his life. It obviously devastated his personal life. Agnes' rejection shocked him so much that he had to make his rethinking of the role of woman in a man's life. This bitter experience remained at his subconscious mind and formulated his ideals. His comment in this regard is noteworthy:

> Any man who allowed himself to suffer from woman had a disease as incurable as cancer...Perhaps a man ought to shoot any woman he planned to leave even if it got him hanged. A less drastic solution would be to 'get so' that no one could hurt you. But by that time as a rule, you were dead.[1]

Hemingway is generally accused of vulgar and obscene themes. But this is not correct. In fact, he was searching for the way out of the social evil the American society was suffering from after the World War I. His novels are evidence of this. Hemingway has produced novels that are fictional sagas of timeless predicament of human sufferings. These novels are true of all societies and of all countries. He has depicted the crisis of human existence in all the ages and generations. Hemingway does not want that man should remain passive to all his sufferings. He wants man to be morally responsible in the situation when God himself was said to be dead. He wants man to be morally more responsible when institutionalized religion is crumbled down and when there is no fear of hell or heaven or social censure. One should not be caught in moral lapses of his own.

The Sun Also Rises, is the first novel in the sequel to the disappointment and disillusionment with which *A Farewell to Arms*, ends. It depicts the phase of the lost generation in which Jake Barnes, the alter-ego of Hemingway, and the protagonist in the novel, carries the scar that symbolizes his crippled spirituality and seeks compensatory sensation in fishing and bull fighting in Spain. In this novel Paris and Spain appear as symbolic counterpoints between which the nights and days are patterned in a sequence to emphasize the moods of gloom and pleasure.

The Sun Also Rises and *A Farewell to Arms* show the mood of withdrawal of the novelist but *For Whom the Bell Tolls* reflects the mood of commitment. Hemingway has shifted his mood to commitment in this novel. Robert Jordan in support of the Republican cause represents political commitment. Hemingway exposes various moods of anti-fascist movement. But more than that the novel is the symbolic expression of the author's love for Spain and its people. Jordan's blowing up of the bridge symbolizes Hemingway's commitment and sacrifice for Spain, the country he loved wholeheartedly.

Old Man and the Sea, shows the spiritual struggle of man to assert his right to live in the world as a man with dignity and not to compromise with life. It also shows that one should not accept defeat under any circumstance. Thus, Hemingway attached more importance to the efforts and the labor than to the ultimate result. Santiago's contribution with the giant fish Marlin and with the sharks shows that Hemingway has deep engrossment in his supreme efforts who never accepts his defeat even though finally he gets only the skeleton of the big fish. *Island in the Stream* reflects the tolling of knell of Hemingway's physical existence. It reflects his sense of total disintegration and irresponsible attitude towards death wish, which comes on the surface of the Gulf Stream. *The Sun Also Rises,* which was published a year before the publication of *A Farewell to*

Arms, projects later phase of Hemingway's experience and shows his concern with the aftermath of the war. This novel is Hemingway's experience regarding his active involvement in the war. His final surrender to death wish is expression to in the *Island in the Stream.* Hemingway was not acquainted with *Nihilism* when First World War broke out. He had not yet abandoned all his illusion, values and aspirations which were associated with the words like honor, sacrifice, glory etc., they needed to be tested on the crucible of experience to find their validity for him. War and love offered him appropriate answer for testing out their validity. Hemingway tested them in *A Farewell to Arms*, through his protagonist Frederic Henry, who is placed in the arena of war. The results are horrible. He is now disillusioned and frustrated with the so-called glories of the world. Only death and destruction emerge as the only bidding reality against which all ideas and aspirations sound hallow. Love turns out to be illusive diversion. This illusion is vividly depicted in *The Sun Also Rises,* which portrays human despair and disillusionment. It also shows how in the context of war man develops the sense of futility of human endeavor. In the metaphysical vision this novel seems to have projected man as pitted against some invisible forces beyond his control. When individual goes through the possible course of life he realizes the futility of his endeavor against the cosmic forces, which rule the universe without any respect for human endeavor or human aspirations and human ideals. If one takes challenge and ventures to go against these forces he has to pay the price for it. Catherine Barkley and Frederic Henry in *A Farewell to Arms,* accepted the challenge and paid the heavy price; Catherine dies in childbirth and for Frederic it is spiritual death.

Hemingway lived in the period of crisis and difficulties. Through Robert Jordan in the *For Whom the Bell Tolls,* he says that we are born into the times of great difficulties. He advocated the masculine society and lived never without women. His novels reflect trends prevalent in the contemporary American society where survival seemed to be difficult. Even in different times one has to learn to survive. Many Christians believe in this philosophy. Such people are called existentialists. Christians believed that Jesus also was existentialist because he put such a premium on individualism and refused to be absorbed into the religious traditions of his father. Shakespeare's *Hamlet* was inordinately concerned about the meaning and tone of man's existence and has received critical interpretation from an existentialist viewpoint. David Thoreau established himself at Walden in order to come to terms with the question of existence and to see what a man might learn from living in the purified state. In almost every age, in fact, there has probably been some one who might be called as existentialist.

All existentialists attempt to establish a separate identity of the individual, which can be viewed as rehabilitation of man in his own eyes. Hemingway's time was very dreadful and appeared to be threatening to swallow up the individual. As John Killinger has pointed out:

> In Hemingway's philosophy nothing has a meaning except survival and existence. The superfluity of culture, race, tradition, even religion, all disappear in the face of one overpowering fact-the necessity to exist on an individual basis. This is the separate peace, the only peace which can be won in our time.[2]

Hemingway saw in his time that death is hovering everywhere: death of ants, grasshoppers, fish, hyenas, kudos, horses, bull and so many other small creatures. He found death lurking over soldiers: the death in Italy, in Cuba, in Africa, in Spain and so on. He saw death in childbirth, death by suicide, death alone and death in-group, selfish death, sacrificing death and graceful death. There is no escape from death. Under this predicament the only way is the separate peace for existence.

There is a sequel of wounds suffered by the individual. Hemingway writes about wounds from the beginning of his career as a writer. The two collections of Hemingway's short stories *In Our Time* and *Men Without Women* contain stories, which are mostly about wounds and physical sufferings caused either by war or by some other kind of violence. Nick Adams the protagonist undergoes and experiences all kinds of violence and receives wounds both physically and psychologically. Jake Barnes in *The Sun Also Rises,* Frederic Henry in *A Farewell to Arms,* Col. Cantwell in *Across the River and Into the Trees,* suffer wound physically and psychologically. Therefore, they long for separate peace. Harry Morgan in *To Have and Have Not,* goes to the extent of murder of his shipmate to protect himself. Thus, they adopt the individualistic approach to protect the self. When god is overthrown and the world is without values, then the rebel must set up his own law and moral code.[3] They live by the motto better to die on our own feet than to live on our knees; better to live one day as a lion than a hundred years as a sheep.

Although Hemingway wrote mostly about death and violence, his attitude towards these themes changed, as he grew old and matured. His later novels have their protagonists placed in wider social context, so that they become representatives of the social groups they belong to. Individualism, however, never deserts his protagonist totally. In *Across the River and Into the Trees,* Cantwell, the protagonist, recoils into his personal world after a series social encounters and makes separate peace with his beloved Renata.

To Have and Have Not is the novel about the impact of economic depression of 1930. This novel vividly describes irresistible spirit of American youth drawn towards Marxism. At the same time, analysis of the human mind in the context of the economic depression, assumes considerable importance in the Hemingway fiction. The impact of the new psychology on Hemingway is well brought out through the following words:

> The contributions of Freud and Jung lies in providing several leading ideas of discussion of the period, which cover the sexual impulses, suppress desires complexes. Hemingway exhibits the Freudian influence in his free and frank discussion of sex.[4]

Hemingway writes about violence because he knew it closely. *A Farewell to Arms* and *For Whom the Bell Tolls* are the best, the novels, which demonstrate violence associated with war. There is a thrill of emotions and actions in both. The tragic destruction of innocence and the richer and deeper exploration of sophisticated mind make both the novels representative of time to which they belong. The doom, pathos and futility of war has been suggested by Hemingway in *A Farewell to Arms*. Frederic Henry and Catherine Berkley are always surrounded by the haunting presence of war, its magnitude, madness, horrible pain and futility. This novel is an account of an individual consciousness of the killing, which is meaningless. Hemingway became uninterested in such killing and diverted his attention to the ritual killing. He appreciated ritual killing like hunting, fishing and bull fighting. As he loved action he found it abundantly in the ritual killing, which is also full of thrill. Actions provide satisfaction to Hemingway and he associates it with manhood and virility.

Birth is associated with life but death is also present in it. This concept has been shown in, *In Our Time*. Birth is new hope and spiritual renewal of life but there is danger associated with it; the danger of death. *Indian Camp,* describes this concept and emphasizes upon the emotional impact of it with a tone of repressed fear and terror. Hemingway's sense of disintegration and the death wish is well expressed in *Island in the Stream*. The book shows the author's increasing obsession with death and disintegration. It is a psychic dream and increasing preoccupation with death. There is a hiatus between the physical activity and the emotional state painted in this novel.

Hemingway was a modernist who was influenced by the theories of Sigmund Freud's analysis of the human mind. This influence is obvious in *The Sun Also Rises,* the novel reveals the war that occurs within the human mind. The war pertains to: "to be religious or no-religious." Jake Barnes goes to the church to pray but he cannot concentrate upon the prayer. He walks out of the cathedral, under the hot sun, which symbolizes his unwillingness to be guided by God. He is an anthropocentric, a degenerated man. Through this novel Hemingway wants to convey to the world that in America there is a generation of young men, which is spiritually sterile. Barnes prefers communicating with Brett Ashley rather than with God. His concerns are more human than divine. He is obviously the one who suffers from the loss of religious faith. He is wounded physically as well as spiritually. Jake Barnes is a typical Hemingway hero, the one who belongs to the *lost generation.* Woman is the cause of Barnes' sufferings. When he removes woman from his mind he feels relieved. Jake Barnes' tragedy is the result of impotency caused by war. He is obsessed with the thought of his inability to satisfy a woman sensually or derives the same satisfaction himself. Jake is relieved and at case only when he removes woman out of his mind. Reynolds has put it better "the sexually incapable man and the sexually active woman—a punishment that might have come from Dante's Inferno."[5] Through Jake Barnes Hemingway tries to convey that the world is basically rotten. Jake being wounded in a rotten way is representative of this rotten world. This shows the general state of the universe. Hemingway, through this novel tries to convey the belief that he is not anti-religious but the nature of his religion is different. Instead of getting entangled with the worldly relations Hemingway proposes to concentrate directly on God. This will cure man of his physical and psychological wounds. Lewis observes that "*The Sun Also Rises* presents romantic love as sick; here the only love which is still healthy is agape, brotherly love."[6] Agape is that universal love which binds man to man. It is a unifying force, which transcends the boundaries of sexual attraction. The novel offers a sort of evolution in Jake's personality. He rises from the sick, rotten man to the level of the universal man. He achieves manhood even though his male equipment does not work.

The sickness of the American society continues to haunt Hemingway in novels like *A Farewell to Arms*. The doom, pathos, and futility of the human life, particularly during war times is a major theme of the novel. The couple in the novel is caught in the maelstrom of war and tries to shield from haunting horror by wrapping in the illusion of violent love. Even in Switzerland, after the Caporetto retreat, the couple is shadowed by the doom of war and engulfed by it. The inevitable sinister destiny of the lovers gets caught in the shattering disillusionment of war and this is the message of this novel for the lovers. The artist in Hemingway was profoundly influenced as well as shaped by his war experiences, both as a participant and as a war correspondent. He explained this in his introduction to the 1948 edition of *A Farewell to Arms,* as a novel, which is conventionally regarded as one that is concerned with themes of love and war.

Hemingway's changed attitude towards life comes through *Old Man and the Sea.* The novel symbolizes that there is a reason to believe in man's ability to withstand the forces of destruction and failure. He can, even under pressure, show grace, courage and fortitude. Santiago, the old man, often feels intimidated by the sea, but, ironically, the sea itself becomes a source of courage with which he fights against the giant fish. The sea, for him, is a life force operating within his frail body and with which he puts stiff resistance against the hostile waves. Santiago is in love with the sea, and since there is no female character in the novel, the sea itself assumes a female role.

Hemingway is often charged of neglecting woman in his artistic vision. Like Herman Melville, the 19th-century American novelist whose *Moby Dick* has no woman character, Hemingway also produced a novel—*The Old Man and the Sea*—which has no woman character at all, and where action takes place, again as in *Moby Dick,* on the sea. It was for this novel that Hemingway was awarded the Nobel Prize in 1954. The Nobel Prize speech by the secretary of the Swedish Academy throws sufficient light on the broadness of Hemingway's artistic vision:

> Within the frame of sporting tale, a moving perspective of man's destiny is opened up. The story is a tribute to the fighting spirit, which does not give in even if the

> marginal gain is nil, a tribute to the moral victory in the midst of defeat.[7]

The novel does not display or exercise the male power, as it is often misunderstood by the feminists today, but projects man's stoicism—his capacity to endure and willingness to die for the objective he has chosen. Incidentally, it is a man-Santiago, an old man for that matter; it could have been a woman—like Tess in Thomas Hardy's celebrated novel *Tess of the d'Urbervilles,* who stoically struggles against the providence and dies in the end.

Hemingway believes in ordinary man's stoicism who shows toughness in the face of death. He believes that men are capable to reveal positive qualities when they are faced with tragic situation. He has given expression to these ideals in bull fighting and hunting, which again are misunderstood as an exercise of the male power. The bullfighter and hunters are common men whose courage and toughness is associated with the profession they follow. Hemingway's concerns as a novelist, are the concerns of the common man. This is an inevitable aspect of the modernist literature in Europe as well as in America. Hemingway is a writer of high modernism in America, follows those trends meticulously, rather, these trends come to his creative genius as naturally as the surrounding factors affecting a man, of creativity. The Hemingway hero is essentially a common man, a bullfighter, a soldier, an old fisherman, and a writer of a common concern lying sick in the hills of Killimanjaro etc. This common man is trapped in deterministic elements. He must offer a bloody fight against the wild bull because that is how he earns wages; he must participate in the destructive war because he cannot escape it, he must endure against the hostile circumstances on the sea because he cannot accept humiliation of returning empty handed. This common man reveals remarkable capacity to endure, and willingness to die for what he thinks he must achieve. He loves his objective, and puts all his efforts to gain it—undergoes tremendous labor—and finally dies. The tragedy evokes deep emotional response—as intense as the tragedy of King Oedipus or of King Lear, or of Prince Hamlet. Hemingway's inclination towards tragedy is revealed in his statement—*all stories if continued far enough, end in the death.* This becomes his theory of tragedy. If the story continues the hero of the story is destroyed by degrees and therein lies a deplete and defeat of man. It is this fear of loss that motivates Nick Adams decision, not to fish the swamp in, *The Big Two Hearted River.* The swamp is made female by its almost anatomical description and Nick Adams' fishing is described as tragic. In *The Three Day Blow,* after having returned from war Nick tries to regenerate himself; he does so by fishing in the two-hearted river but he is afraid of undertaking action of fishing in the swamp for it would be tragic. Swamp being female, demands action and the action depletes man. It appears as if Hemingway believes that women cause tragedy by diminishing the psychic reserves, by dying and damaging the male's sole. This is the point of the Major's advise in *In Another Country,* where the Major's wife has died and his psychic loss is symbolized by his withered hand. Woman also tangle the male in debilitating domestic concerns, the image of the eagle caught with a canvas decoy in *Fathers and Sons,* and women lure the male away from the familiar scope of experience as the *riau-riau,* Maera from the concentration on the bull fight. The net result of all this is implied by the title of *Hills Like White Elephants,* in which the bulge of pregnancy likened to a white elephant, a gift calculated to make the recipient bankrupt. In sum, woman's ultimate end is the essential catastrophe for the male, making him bankrupt, empty of any reserves. Even though the male is the central figure in *The Sun Also Rises,* Brett Ashley, a woman is painted as tough and complicated woman, which fits in the 'iceberg' theory. She is closely connected with the *riau-riau* dance. This novel is a tragedy. The basic motif in this novel is the "dear financial basis" which is upset by the carnival atmosphere of the Feria. This exchange motif also applied to the sexual and psychological relationships. Brett's fiancé Mike is bankrupt both financially and spiritually. Romero's involvement with Brett leads to "defeat" in the fight with Cohn, but Romero is not destroyed; he fights back. Later, by concentrating on the bullfight, he regains energy, even though, still in love with Brett. Romero has momentarily gained but, in Hemingway's view, this gain can only be temporary. Jake Barnes' wound is his first tragedy but Brett diminishes Jake too. She makes no sexual demands upon Jake but she makes spiritual demands, since the wound leaves Jake capable of love in all except in physical sense. This novel is the expression of one of the most pessimistic view, ever expressed in literature. It expresses the exchange value of life. One has to give something and get something else in return.

A Farewell to Arms is the novel of pessimism from another angle. It is centered around sexual exchange. Frederics Henry rejects war and brothel in exchange of domestic life and romantic love but ends in tragedy. The death of Catherine is not to be construed as the tragedy of Catherine. It is the tragedy of Frederic Henry as he suffers loss and sustains shattering traumatic effect of Catherine's loss. She burdens him with responsibility and diminishes his psychic energy. As the couple advances to get more into the domestic life it gets trapped. The couple's crossing the lake arriving to cold Switzerland; Catherine allowing her hair to grow longer; leaving hotel and moving to the cottage etc. symbolize couple's getting into domestic life. But all that culminates is ultimately the tragic end of romantic love. Catherine finds herself trapped biologically. Frederic Henry finds himself wounded once again—this time spiritually.

Hemingway's attitude towards woman remained ambivalent till late. It was only recently after the publication *The Garden of Eden* that Hemingway's generous attitude to humanity including woman came to be known. His earlier woman characters however, are traditionally drawn. In *To Have and Have Not,* he presents Marie as stupid but not malicious, wholly devoted to her husband, though ex-whore but possesses the heart of gold. However, she and her children become part of force, which derive Morgan to loss in his attempt to gain economic freedom, which ultimately results into Morgan's death. *Snows of Killimanjaro* is a story of writer getting corrupt. Harry, the writer, attempts to join the rank of riches and becomes corrupt by selling himself out to a rich lady. As a result he abandons his art of writing and adapts to materialism. Helen, his wife, though admirably good lady in character and duty to her husband, has the cunningness of hyena. This may be perhaps because the other hidden characters of hers are kept underwater according to the author's "iceberg" theory which cannot be so easily surfaced. He attempts to put all blame upon her as responsible to destroy his art of writing. In the short story *The Short Happy Life of Francis Macomber,* Margot Macomber is shown as a woman who cannot tolerate her husband as a powerful man. When he tries to become transformed from hen-pecked husband to a brave man he is killed at her instance. *For Whom the Bell Tolls,* on the other hand, is the novel where the woman is shown more loving and faithful. Maria's love with Robert Jordan is therapeutic. The love, which erases Maria's past, helps Jordan resolve his ambivalence to war for the republic cause. He rejects his domestic life and his profession of teaching for his larger duty of commitment of larger cause. Earl Rovit's observation in this regard is interesting. He observes that there are two sets of women in the novel. One is a threatening mother and a purified daughter-lover—Pilar. She smells the odor of semen, which symbolizes birth and death both, of man. She is a threat to Jordan as she wants to absorb the identity of the lovers by manipulation of their fates. The other set of women is the loving women, represented by Maria. Her love offers relief to the man she loves. This novel offers the wandering thoughts of the protagonist, Jordan. His attitude towards Maria changes as his thought wanders. The novel offers pessimistic view of life. In his commitment to larger objective for the republic cause, Jordan's death becomes inevitable in the blowing of the bridge and the blowing of bridge is inevitable to which he has made a serious and sincere commitment. There is also another angle to the story, which relates to division of labor. Women cook and men make plans. However, the male-female relationship shown in the novel is only temporary affair, not lasting. This relationship would drain out the male's psychic and sexual resources. The stored semen symbolizes life and the spent semen symbolizes the death. In the novel Jordan's sexual act with Maria, which is temporary, drains out the semen, which indicates that his death is certain.

Across the River and Into the Trees offers the view that the female can rejuvenate the male and can give the new birth or new lease of life to man. Renata is similar to Maria who offers her love to the old Colonel Cantwell and offers him a rebirth as her name suggests. She offers the dying Colonel his vitality. This novel includes several of Hemingway's own psychological quirks. The imagery of death persists here also. The girl Renata ostensibly allows Colonel Cantwell to rejuvenate through his death. It is like the decoy hen luring male duck to his death. Hemingway therefore reflects his ambivalence towards the female characters he had portrayed.

Old Man and the Sea does not include any female character. The sea is the only female in the novel and the sea is at once Santiago's life source, field of combat and the foe as well. In the opinion of Keiichi Harada, sea could become a feminine universe in which Santiago undertakes action to gain a prize, the Marlin with which he is so completely identifies himself. The action, which makes Santiago, an enduring hero in his heroic attempt to gain what lies beyond the reach of all, as, at the same time, associated with Santiago's supreme gain. Unencumbered by the necessity to characterize a female Hemingway has found an objective correlative, which illustrates the nature of man's opponent. The novelist even portrays Santiago as loving the sea, since the threatening aspects have been objectified symbolically. In *Island in the Stream,* written at or near the same time, the women are flat characters again, with no noteworthy or remarkable traits of their personality. His views about women remain highly personal, which makes them rather ambivalent and at times even disputable.

Hemingway never drew a full female character, however the men in his works are not the central figures. The male female exchange is a threat to the conservation of self, since action must be undertaken and action leads to disaster; female is a threat because she draws the male from prescribed limitations of experience. This is why, Cayctano stays away from woman. The movement from withdrawal to action and the consequent loss becomes tragic. The loss is inevitable but the action must be undertaken. Courtly love is irrelevant in the modern world. However, love is not to be rejected out rightly. Hemingway's vast reading of romance gives him enough insight to write about the women and war. Courtly love indicates revealingly enough that women were a kind of lesser substitute for work. Women provide the local discipline only. *The Sun Also Rises,* is reminiscent of the situation in a medieval romance. For Hemingway, the tradition may no longer work in the modern world. But the traditional courtly love has not been called into question and the forces, which have tried to undermine the effectiveness of this tradition, has come under criticism. This novel presents an indictment of the modern woman who makes true knighthood of impossible goal for the modern man. Modern man cannot be a knight. He falls short of the ideal. Jake Barnes is critical of his own shortcomings. Modern technological warfare also reveals itself as an enterprise, which is something less than noble and which no longer offers modern man the opportunity to act in knightly fashion. So it is indicted too. But this indictment, of the modern woman, modern warfare and to a lesser degree modern man, must not be misinterpreted as an indictment of the courtly love and chivalric traditions. Rather, in revealing the ineffectiveness of knightly behaviour in the modern world, Hemingway is exhibiting the nostalgia for the days when such behaviour was properly rewarded because courtly love and chivalric traditions were successful as system of values.

> It is an ironic commentary on the modern world and perhaps even on modern man, that Jake is transformed into the ideal knight by an accident of modern war rather than by a moral choice. Nonetheless, Jake seems more or less satisfied by the behaviour possible for him. This behaviour is similar to the love 'par amours' and 'pure love' which according to D.W. Robertson, was

> considered acceptable for a knight; 'love par amours' was 'a love for the sight of the beloved which may lead to a kiss or a chaste (not nude) embrace...(but, whose) chief satisfaction arises from the contemplation of the beauty of the beloved, and 'pure love' was 'the kiss', the embrace and contact with the nude beloved but with the final solace omitted.[8]

One can find the significance of *The Sun Also Rises* clearly when one reads the *Death in the Afternoon,* which is a collection of non-fiction essays in which Hemingway asserts that the bullfight is not a sport but a tragedy, which is well ordered and strongly disciplined by ritual and that the aficionado, or the lover of the bullfight may be said to be one who has this sense of the tragedy and ritual of the fight. Hemingway's sense of the relationship between the bullfight and the tragedy and his evident admiration for a ritual which esthetically shapes passion in particular the passion for death, which is one of the two things that are necessary for a country to love bullfights. Modern woman in this novel is shown as fickle minded as Brett rejects one lover after another. Consequently, this modern woman is also rejected by all the lovers and finally Jake alone remains her best friend, the true knight in the chivalric tradition. The novel depicts the distorted version of courtly orders of love. This is one of the several secrets of society to which man belongs. Of course, several societies appear constantly in Hemingway's fiction and occur in several oft-noted manifestations. Though a number of medieval knights might dedicate themselves to a single lady and thereby enroll in the courtly order of the love, the lady must, grant favor to the single man, the most worthy knight. The knight to whom she grants this favor has the duty to secrecy, for her reputation is of great concern. Erich Auerbach suggests that the knights so enrolled have the sense that they are set off, as members of an elected society, from the mass of common humanity. Brett is not worthy of such order of love; the order that is dedicated to her necessarily deviates radically from these above stated principles. This calamity of civilization resulted out of the First World War, affects the lives of nearly all characters in the novel in a negative way. Jake is the permanently most of all, affected as he is wounded and his wound is a horror. This break with the chivalric tradition, in which the strength, courage and integrity of individual knights determined the outcome of battles, has occurred for centuries but, did not occur decisively until modern technological advances took hold in twentieth century. Such a wound, however devastating personally, looks like the nobility of glorious death in the battle. This kind of death one might expect to meet the chivalric combat. But even when death comes on the battlefield it presents itself in a ignoble guise. Modern warfare is indicted because it makes knightly behaviour impossible for the modern man. Same is the case of modern woman of the post war period like Brett, who makes the knightly behaviour of modern man impossible.

A *Farewell to Arms* and *Across the River and into the Trees* including *For Whom the Bell Tolls,* present modern knights struggling to behave in accordance with medieval traditions. *The Sun Also Rises,* presents both the chivalric knight in the war and the courtly knight in the love relationship. The focus of these novels is on the protagonists' role, as chivalric knights, but have experience only of a limited success on the battlefield. They are able to dedicate themselves to ladies who actually do approximate the medieval ideal lady. The modem knights therefore again a measure of satisfaction from their courtly, behaviour. Hemingway's nostalgia for the courtly love tradition results then either in the creation of Brett Ashley, a modern woman who is vividly real though presented sympathetically, or Catherine Barkley, Maria, Renata, the modern woman who are one dimensional though presented sympathetically but not real. They are seldom both, the sympathetic and real. Hemingway's male protagonists are always presented sympathetically; their flaws, failures, self-pity, all is justified, at least within the text, because these are men with the expectations and the sensibilities of the Middle Ages who must live as Hemingway would expect, *In Our Time.*

The Hills Like White Elephants is a short story, which reveals the truth that is universally acknowledged. A man, who has impregnated a woman he does not love, rapidly loses his zest for her. The man repeats his reasons for the girl to have an abortion and restore unhampered life style but the girl does not agree. She does not want to go for the abortion on his terms. She has the real chance to avoid the abortion and pushes the argument to new limits that her lover can neither comprehend nor reach. The girl's name Jig, sounds like Hemingway's compromise between the Elizabethan *Jug Jug* and the modern French 'zig zig' terms for coitus. She becomes conscious of what girl means to the American. When she reveals her pregnancy to him she becomes instantly white elephant in his eyes. White elephant a once prized possession has lost its former value in America and acquires symbolic complexity. The unwanted pregnancy for the awful daring of a moment's surrender (the waste land), which the Americans believe an abortion can retreat.

The Hills Like White Elephant is of course an extraordinary example of modernist writing, of the use of the suggestive fragment, of omission and elision, of making the reader do much of the work in comprehending the story. Attempts to analyze even short passages of the dialogue produce pages of prose.[9]

Several critics have seen a dynamic element in the story. The dynamism is that the girl Jig agrees to abortion but not on terms of her lover boy; she does go for the abortion and after having abortion she leaves the boy. This dynamics was not very much appreciated by the critics. The boy did not consider the reality of a child. The girl of course had this realization and feels that the boy had considered neither the child nor her own choice. The story has autobiographical elements, as Hemingway's assumed involvement in it is obvious. The American position to the pregnancy was really Hemingway's belated desire to thwart the birth of his first son. This story had been written when Hemingway was on his honeymoon with Pauline Pfeiffer. But Jig is identified with Hadley, and it is difficult to screen out the motivation of Hemingway in it.

Somewhere in the dialogue the idea comes to the mind of Jig that fetus and she both have become white elephant to her lover. White elephant is the romantic element of Eastern legend in which it is considered as sacred beast, prized possession and the Americans have no ability of this possession. The Americans are not worthy of this sacred prized possession for they have lost their values and have become the selfish people. This scared animal cannot remain with the unworthy Americans. The girl finds alternative when she walks to the end of the plantation and into the sunlight, which symbolizes her disillusionment and seeks a light of wisdom that is sunlight. The boy forces her to consent to operation in order to regain his love. This stirs her to a new level of response, which begins when she walks to the end of the plantation and into the sunlight. For the first time standing alone, she sees the sharp contrast in the landscape: the sterile, brown countryside (the abortion) to her right and the fertile fields (the child) to her left. It can be concluded point that her visionary landscape of the hills vanish behind the more pictorial, one of the grain fields, the fulfillment which she will lose by agreeing to the abortion. The clouds, which moved across the field of grain, signal the death of the fetus. However the girl has her apparent alternatives. This story reveals that the American male does not want to face situation, which is the creation of his own. He turns sex into an entertainment and then a convenience for himself without consulting the woman's wishes or needs. In the story she will have abortion of her own choice. Romance is whiteness and Jig being considered is a playgirl whom the boy does not want to resume. Hemingway was also influenced by Karl Marx's philosophy of human civilization. This is evident in *The Sun Also Rises*. The novel emphasizes Marx's economic philosophy. This philosophy is about the use of surpluses. Scott Donaldson calls it "morality of compensation". Hemingway explores here the central concern indirectly through apparent trifles. Jake is drinking enough to get his money's worth but he is drinking for wrong reasons, not joyfully but commercially. Bill Gorton's expenditure is lavish which disturbs Jake. However, he aligns Bill with the financial carelessness of

Brett and Mike rather than meticulousness of himself. The redundant shoeshine Bill buys and Bill's buying stuffed dogs disturb Jake. This novel, therefore, can be called the morality of surplus rather than the morality of compensation. This presents the concept of exchange value. Surplus gradually becomes ambivalent when the tendency of spending exceeds. This becomes than the source of destruction. Jake fears and becomes literally and figuratively gun shy. War, on the large scale, pervasively figures the destructive use of surplus through out the novel. A colossal cultural over-reaching into too much wealth, power, greed, in the name of patriotism; this obviously is the impact of war which wrecked the lives of a generation. This war has stripped away its excess in self-destruction leaving a kind of nothingness at its center, a lack figured most clearly in Jake's wound. *The Sun Also Rises* suggests therefore, the proper balance between the financial spending and the moral values. One should not go in excess of what his limit permits. Jake, however, after the destruction of the war, alternatively fears about it and desires this excess to be eliminated.

The novel maps his alternative advances into and retreat from this tenuous ground into and from the terrain of the bull. Jake makes a difference in simple exchange and just exchange of value. Just exchange is equitable exchange as against the simple exchange. Just exchange is legal, correct, proper, exact, accurate, uniform exchange. Simple exchange is foolish exchange. This exchange of vale arises in the buying of stuffed dogs by Bill Gorton, which according to Jake is not just expenditure. A person can balance both the financial and moral checkbook and Jake suggests that one should do so to get the money's worth. This just spending and simple spending is the moral center of the novel. But in such a wretched, pitiful, and foolish imbalance lies the humanity of Jake when he rescues Brett in conventional sexual equation of one to one (1+1), without a penis, (he has received a bullet there, in the war). This nothingness that lies with Jake and he strikes a balance between this nothingness. The relationship with Brett that Jake has with nothingness contains the humanity and morality.

Old Man and the Sea is Hemingway's personal experience of fishing. In 1934, Hemingway had purchased a thirty-eight foot cabin cruise and named it *Pilar* after the pet name for his wife Pauline. Living in the Key West, the author was aware of the wonderful Marlin fishing to be found around Bimini and he planned to use the *Pilar* for Fishing expedition. Hemingway had invited his friend Henry Mike to join in Key West for his long awaited fishing. He was artist and lived in Ogunquit Maine. He used to spend winter in West Palm Beach, painting and fishing. He was an experienced fisherman and had launched the sport of tuna fishing on rod and reel in the New England Coastal waters, landing sixteen giant tuna in the summer of 1933. Starter recalled:

> Hem talked me into going with him to Bimini, fishing and sharing the experiences of running *Pilar*. The deal was that I would fish one side of the boat and Hem the other. We fished for black marlin off Bimini for almost a month, and did not even get a strike. Then one day we decided to troll at a faster speed and I snagged a big one.[10]

This served as model for Hemingway's 1952 Pulitzer Prize winning novel *Old Man and the Sea,* which was also considered as outstanding by Swedish Academy when he was awarded the Nobel Prize in 1954.

The Garden of Eden is about a woman trying to destroy a largely good man in vain. David Bourne, well-qualified man, longs for happy and productive life. He was a former First World War ace pilot and a son of West African hunter and a successful writer. Catherine, the beautiful and wealthy woman who married him, tries to reduce the differences between them by cajoling him into assuming her name and a feminine role in bed. She also makes him appear feminine as close to her as possible. She also tries to unman him as a writer. David flees his wife's attempt to destroy him as a male with a sure sense of his sexual and vocational identity by imaginatively fleeing into an all-male terrain. Catherine burns his stories and tries to devastate his terrain. In this novel, Hemingway has combined the meticulous account of woman's descent into psychosis but with some sympathy for her situation. He has felt the complexity of the woman in this novel and in Catherine's characterization. Hemingway has shown compassion for her strange, sexual desires. This suggests in Hemingway the rudiments of feminist perspective. Catherine wishes she were a boy. Her attempt to destroy her husband David is flamboyantly clear as her deepening madness. Catherine's desires though are paean (song of praise), but these desires make her most menacing member of the gallery of threatening women in Hemingway's fiction.

According to Lynn, Hemingway's mother tried to convince herself and others that 'Ernest and Marceline, his older sister by eighteen months, were twine of the same sex'. Consequently, Lynn's argument runs, Hemingway was unsure of whether he was male or some blend of male and female and the swaggering macho stances which so characterized his adult life were a desperate attempt to hide from the world his androgynous longings. Lynn's thesis helps to explain a great deal of Hemingway the androgynous longing which are so obviously dramatized in *The Garden of Eden,* the macho behaviour, the much greater tolerance of lesbians than homosexuals, the obsessive concern with hair length that surfaces in so many works and much more... The psyche that produced *A Farewell to Arms* and the novel itself were capacious enough to accommodate the claim of both Lewis and Lynn...he confronted the androgynous yearning which are so clearly dramatized in *The Garden Of Eden,* with for example, David's assuming the name of Catherine during intercourse and apparently telling himself somehow be sodomised.[11]

In *A Farewell to Arms*, to surrender to feminine does not follow from experimenting with forbidden sexual techniques but with forsaking male identity as it is defined in the earlier novels. The male should be skillful and successful in his play as well as in his work and the sexual quest is one of the games he plays; winning strengthens the victor's sense of himself as forceful separate male. The feminine component of the male self is opposed to all of this.

A Farewell to Arms is a twin tale of love and war. The protagonists are psychically prepared for their blending by two artillery shells; one blows to bits the man to whom Catherine was engaged and the other wounds Henry to whom she loved. This novel reflects the denial of male activity to the author, that is, the recruitment in the army and, therefore, he takes here the longer desertion for which he was not born or made. He has, therefore, reflected his feelings through the protagonist Henry who rejects the world of guns around and takes interest in drinking, merry-making. Hemingway is of the view that the shorthaired women destroy men and this has been clear from the role of Brett in *The Sun Also Rises* and Catherine Bourne of *The Garden of Eden. A Farewell to Arms* shows that one can escape war of guns but he cannot escape the larger war of existence that is life. If one attempts to do so, death is the only alternative. It also analyses the concept of *nada*, as all of Catherine's admirable attributes are irrelevant as she dies. This novel tells that women nurtures man but eventually kills him. Catherine gives birth to a baby who is dark, long and wise as Henry, nurtures him and then kills him though unintentionally. The child symbolizes the perilous future of Henry's manhood apparently nurtured by Catherine but fated to be killed by her, by entanglement and something, if she survives. One is better off with nada and grief in facing them. This also symbolizes that man can assume God-like role and exercise power of giving death as he can give birth. The novel further reveals that nature's destruction is all pervasive; love is its treatment particularly in the world of chaos.

A Farewell to Arms has a conspicuous reference to religion. It is significant that when a generation of young Americans had felt a loss of religious faiths, Hemingway thinks of necessity to invoke religious feelings. When Henry leaves for the front Catherine gives him a Saint Anthony medal. This means Saint Anthony is invoked for the return of lost property of Catherine, namely, Frederic Henry; protection of the pregnancy; protection of Henry. This indicates that man has to visit society for his protection. Thus, the religious motif present in the novel suggests that a visit to Abrussi, a place of honor and dignity for a man is very significant. This will give him love for God and his own protection, happiness and well-being. This choice of place made by Hemingway in this novel signifies his association with religion, internally. He, therefore, gives importance to that aspect of society, which has been significant for centuries. There is invocation of saints and religion in the novel against hydrophobia, epilepsy and nervous disorder. It appears that Hemingway had read about the saints like, a daily newspaper. This invocation helps in a sense when Frederic escapes sudden death, at the bridge and rises above water opposite San Vito.

A Farewell to Arms, is also the study of a twentieth century multiplicity in which there appears a broken neck of a modern man. The modern man has to face the chaotic forces of the twentieth century with an age and place of faith. Thus, it appears that Hemingway's writing is from the heart of a Christian tradition. Frederic Henry in the novel thinks that let the soul live on the servant's loss, on the loss of the body and let the body pine or grieve so long as the soul increases its riches. We owe God death and death is swallowed up in victory. Thus, Hemingway shows much concern for death and the conditions of the soul. The main focus of the novel becomes obvious when Frederic is shown coming to terms with suffering and of Catherine, to accept the reality of life that there is a suffering and that there is no escape from it. Death is the only escape. Frederic suffers with Catherine and his final epiphany resides in the knowledge that it is love that has devised the torment. Hemingway has captured the mood of time showing concern as to where will man go when he has no future, where will he go when his dear ones are dead; when everything becomes unreal to him. This makes Hemingway the most representative of his times. He captures with remarkable effectiveness, the helplessness and spiritual barrenness, his generation felt and experienced. Thus, he becomes a true representative of the "lost generation."

In the game of sexual politics the American man had lost the power. The woman controls him. The regain of power for him was useless for he is destroyed by his woman. This is vividly painted in the short story of *The Short Happy Life of Francis Macomber.* American woman lost her domesticity. This loss stood in the way of working out a satisfactory sex relationship under the conditions pervading the modern world. The American woman is tired of the position she has won in the struggle for power and dominance. She is tired of her hair brushed back like a boy's. Hemingway feels that she has traded the feminine grace and tenderness for power over man. *Cat in the Rain,* a short story, portrays such a woman. Her search for a kitty in the rain is symbolic of her desire to tie her knot in the back because she has become tired of looking like a boy and wants a simple domestic life of a woman of grace and tenderness. Catherine Barkley has a desire to have a home and family seeking stable relationship with her husband.

In *For Whom the Bell Tolls,* it is a male myth that Hemingway has shown. In this novel Hemingway's woman is extremely docile and submissive. This cannot be possible in the real life. Maria, the loving girl, is the sun driving away the night and abolishing loneliness. She is so simple that she hardly appears to be real. Hemingway himself has realized this and makes Jordan say may be it is like dream you have when someone you have seen in the cinema comes to your bed at night and is so kind and lovely. Hemingway woman like Catherine in *A Farewell to Arms,* and Renata in *Across the River and into the Trees,* are also shown very simple, docile and submissive. Male keeps them in perennial subjugation. Hemingway generally is charged of being a male chauvinist. The feminists interpret that his works serve only half of the humanity. In the words of Nirmal Mukharjee:

> Hemingway's failure to establish the validity from feminist point of view (*He has projected and presented male and male consciousness based on Huckleberry Finn, tradition.* Added by me). Hemingway's failure to draw strong independent, self-fulfilled woman leads to an ultimate failure of his part to realize the great human potential in half the human race.[12]

This view is proved wrong in *The Garden of Eden* where the heroine is a strong, self-willed woman who wants her husband to be submissive to her sexual demands. In bed, she treats him almost 'like a woman, and, in the process, it seems, the whole affair turns into a lesbian one. In fact, it is wrong to label Hemingway as antifeminist. He belongs to that phase of history when violence and brutality marked the time. The America between the two world wars was a nation caught in the internal conflict, when a common American longed for the promises of paradise to come true. It is unlikely that Hemingway should have taken a feminist issue and worked on it at that time. Even most of the woman writers on America at this time—Gertrude Stein, for example, were obsessively concerned with the malaise of modernism. No wonder then that writer like Hemingway who actually participated in war—a major factor responsible for modernism in America—should write about the soldier's issue and deal with them from a soldier's point of view.

Hemingway wrote about unease and instability, which he faced as personal psychology. His unease is that of the individual man, fearful for his own masculinity, oppressed by the need particularly to prove himself. He dwells upon horrible things just to convince himself that 'he can take.' His heroes struggle in endless isolation against heavy odds, but they enjoy their struggle unconventionally and wholeheartedly like Santiago. Hemingway believes that life is full of struggle and that man is not made for defeat. Man can be destroyed but not defeated. There is a treatment of human suffering and death in *For Whom the Bell Tolls*, embraced for the welfare of humanity a conception alien to the early works and this adds to the status of the novel.

Hemingway writes about cosmic order also. In *The Garden of Eden*, Hemingway was preoccupied with cosmic problem. He maintained his philosophy that there should be a proper world order. Man cannot behave like woman and woman like man. He argues, why? Catherine's behaviour like man in this novel by cutting hair, initiating David to another woman and assuming herself the name of David during the course of copulation, Hemingway considers, is the disorder of cosmic nature. For him every one has to be in its proper place for peace and order. Hemingway has written his experiences of the World War I, as well as of the peacetime in, *In Our Time*, of the disorder of the universe. In, *Men Without Women*, he has written the pangs of divorcing Hadley his first wife together with the memory of grandfather's death. He wrote *Winner Takes Nothing*, with the knowledge of his father's suicide and the pain of fractured hand he suffered. *Indian Camp*, the first Nick story in which he has shown his first encounter with death as evil. In the story Nick a very sensitive boy, learns of birth, pain and death when, the Indian father commits suicide, because he could not bear the pain and suffering of his wife during labour, while performing a caesarian with a Jack-knife and sewing it with tapered gut leaders. This was the terrible scene for young Nick. *The Battler* provides another encounter of Nick with evil in the crazy and violent world of a busted prized fighter. *The Killer* shows helpless surrender of Ole Anderson to the killer and Nick suffers shock of death. In *Ten Indian,* Hemingway shows the adjustment of young people wit the problems of early life and love, which is an another shock. The invitation to love and sex when one enters young manhood in *The End of Something* creates fear of consequences. Love was fun earlier but it leads to marriage, seeking job and other responsibilities. Man does not want to share these responsibilities. In *Now I lay Me,* he has overcome his fear of telling the war time experiences directly. He reveals that 'he cannot sleep in darkness, if he does so, his soul will go away never to return.' In *The Soldier's Home,* Hemingway shows that he is now disillusioned with war. He cannot go back to the old values. He breaks his relation with his mother also. War is no longer the place to show heroism and valor and prowess. In the war man dies like animal and not like man. *One Reader Writes,* shows the conflict of mind when wife is confused whether to have or not to have her husband who gets back to her after years from abroad with syphilis. This is a great awareness of the social values and of the social issues. *A Clean Well Lighted Place,* vividly demonstrated the fear—nada, represented by darkness and shadow which in turn represents evil and gloom of hell, chaos and death. Hope and confidence symbolize light and good life. *Old Man at the Bridge,* presents helplessness of a old man who cannot move ahead because of unsurmountable fatigue and left to the mercy of fascist artillery. He cannot run to the safety like his cats and pigeons in the face of war. He is like goats symbolizing helpless humanity, cannot run for safety. *The Short Happy Life of Francis Macomber* gives expression to the character of the American woman. Though they are good looking, they are predatory. They break the softened man into pieces. American people are unpredictable. They look boys at fifty and their women are killers.

In these short stories Hemingway gives expression to his concern that the universe is not in order. There is imbalance pervading everything. Things are not in their proper place and have no proper nature. Things are out of joint, asserts Hemingway like Hamlet, but does not have Hamlet's inclination to put them in order. He has brought out this cultural chaos in *The Sun Also Rises.*

The Sun Also Rises is the extension of the theme already dealt with earlier in a short story *Soldier's Home.* It is a study of love that does not bear fruit, and does not get fulfilled. The search for joy is frustration. Expectations are belied. There is reckless drinking to submerge frustration. The novel depicts horrible picture of disillusionment in romantic love. There appears a sense of widespread emptiness and everybody is tired of life. The atmosphere of sickness and abnormality contaminates all. Love between man and woman is only a dream. Chronologically, the action in *The Sun Also Rises* anticipates the action in *A Farewell To Arms,* as it deals with the actual war, the effect of which is depicted in both the novels. These two novels assert that the love and war a part of the life of twentieth century American people.

The Fifth Column and *For Whom The Bell Tolls,* shows that the people are no more interested in loving the woman and enjoying the sex life, when it comes to their duty and the responsibility. Philips in *The Fifth Column* gives up his love of Dorothy. Jordan in *For Whom The Bell Tolls* does not take much interest in Maria. Both are serious about their duty and solidarity to all the human beings. *For Whom The Bell Tolls* expresses a mythical love, which is for the entire human society and it is not confined to any individual. This novel suggests choice between two options of life available:

(1) Tyranny and iron rule and

(2) Freedom and good of all, specially, of the poor people.

Old Man And The Sea, presents the view that all living creatures are same in the universe but animals physically is stronger than man. For Hemingway this physical strength is not enough for man. There has to be trickery and cunning in man besides physical strength. Pride in man is not lasting; man loses it before exterior forces. Santiago loses this pride before the elemental strength of marlin and acquires humility. Sharks attack his prize for fortune. Therefore, there has to be maintained a dignity of man and animal both and thereby, create solidarity and fraternity of man and animal. This concept has been very well expressed in this novel.

For Whom The Bell Tolls reveals that the man is totally dependent on nature. At a time human agency of destruction is so powerful that even nature fails to face it. But when nature is in a malignant mood, it brings utter disaster and there is no escape from it. Nature shows her apathy to man by depriving him of any favor. Nature has, not shown favor to Santiago for long by denying any fish for eighty-four days and when he gets a big marlin nature destroys it through sharks. Sharks are, agents of nemesis and disaster. Fish symbolizes unattainable thing. Going too far out to get unattainable thing is trespassing into forbidden territory. This amounts to misadventure for man and Santiago does it and meets the fate for his transgress.

Island in the Stream is the novel, which describes the similar concept. It describes the nature of Infinite Ocean. The Gulf Stream besides standing for the common sea and its qualities stand also for the extra ordinary and strange depth. The idea of oceans being far out where common men do not or dare go. Ocean and the Gulf Stream are connected with the universe, the infinite cosmos that manifest creation. Here lies the principle of life. Nature is not co-operative always to the design of man. Thomas Hudson, who has his temporary boat into a sea for happy and exciting occasion and for underwater fishing, is intimidated by imminent fear of death. Sea is manifestation of the universe, the cosmic principle governing human existence and creation. Nature and sea are the cradle and grave of man, There is no escape of man from them.

Hemingway's novels shed ample light on the state of man in relation with the universe. Man makes struggle with the universe, heroically, unmindful of the consequences of this struggle. However, Hemingway, in his novels expresses a great faith in man's power of tolerance and bravery, facing all odds of life. Love is not visualized merely as bodily or sexual union; he envisages love as union both of the body and the sole. An ideal blend of sex and love open the window to spiritual ecstasy. Love to Hemingway is a second name for religion and it is an excellent blessing of life. If tested even once, it makes the life worthwhile. His love is partly physical and partly platonic and is very close to the concept of love found in metaphysical poetry. True love has tender feelings in which the either of the lovers acts and loves for the other. This sublime love to Hemingway becomes a cosmic phenomenon operating behind the universe. Love in Hemingway's works has individual as well as social implication. Love preoccupied by sexual appetite alone may have adverse social effect and Hemingway is in a mood to censure such love. Love in *For Whom the Bell Tolls,* which produces nobility and height in the character is shown in developed form in, *A Farewell to Arms*. A death of the body does not mean the death of love and of this love there is no happy end if two people love each other truly. This concept has been elaborated in *Death in the Afternoon.* By the time Hemingway comes to write *The Old Man and the Sea,* the concept of his love develops further. It becomes a principle permeating the entire universe and binding the creatures of the earth, the sea and the bodies in the cosmos with the same bond as exists between moon and the sea. Moon is symbolized as male and the sea as female. Moon affects the sea as man does to woman. The sea makes love under the cover of darkness. According to Hemingway man can rise above the physical pleasure of sex—appetite and he can still be a lover of joy of living. Santiago in *The Old Man and the Sea* is above the pleasure of physical sex, and his life is still worth living; and he continues his life struggle, for one reason or another. But in, *A Farewell to Arms* Hemingway holds the view that the true love and the true happiness of life have no long duration. This concept he conveys in the *For Whom the Bell Tolls,* and holds the view that exterior forces come in the way of healthy enjoyment of life and leads to a loss of balance of mankind, which is also shown in *The Sun Also Rises.* War brings about a general dehumanization and loss of dignity of those who are fighting. It brings loss of human affection and filial bond of love between a mother and son. War wounds and pain, the very memory of which keeps soldiers sleepless and causes loss of all old values, moral or religious.

The common theme to all these novels is love and labor. These are the two important factors, which affect the lives of characters in the Hemingway fiction. Initially, love happens to be an attraction between the two opposite sexes but as story progresses this love assumes a form of emotional bond and ultimately it transcends mere physicality. Agape is the term, which can best describe love in the Hemingway fiction as it reached to the climax. Agape demonstrates that form of love which is an expression of adoration for the universality and which comes down gradually to the level of individual. Love as quoted in the dictionary of Biblical theology is a form of divine blessing for all as a group and also for each individual. Love also means suffering. Jesus Christ who loved humanity had to suffer. Similarly, the Hemingway hero suffers for the sake of love. Frederic Henry in *A Farewell to Arms* comes out in the rain in the final scene of the novel as if to demonstrate that love for Catherine has become a love for all those who suffer. Similarly, Jordan in *For Whom the Bell Tolls* has also crossed the boundaries of physical love. He is a defeated man but not demoralized. The Hemingway hero is often involved in personal morality. He is man of conscience and is fully aware of his responsibility in his involvement with whatever he takes up. He knows the consequences and faces them stoically. Stoicism is an important trait of Hemingway hero. He fights against all odds, with remarkable determination even though he is defeated in the end. His involvement is often violent. Games like hunting, bull fighting, which involves violence even brutality, mark the Hemingway world. This has always made the conventional critics charge Hemingway of exercising male power. A proper interpretation will reveal the fact that these brutalities and violent acts exposed the futility of these activities. If Hemingway is a writer of war he is also concerned at the same time with other violent issues, which prove man's futile attempts to gain any profit out of it. This makes Hemingway again writer of labor, which can be discerned, in the ceaseless efforts on the part of Hemingway hero to gain his objective. In the present context labor has wider connotation and different sheds of meanings. It is pangs of childbirth as in the case of Catherine and at the same time tenacity of efforts to achieve one's goal as in the case of Santiago in *The Old Man and the Sea.* The ultimate tragedy is the result of these two factors. Love and labor are the very essence of the Hemingway fiction.

Agape is described as "that highest and noblest form of love which sees some thing infinitely precious in its object."[13] The Hemingway hero always finds in his love something more precious than everything else in the world. He ceases to be a mere lover boy, but the one involved in the total anatomy of love. He ceases to be a man who is attracted towards the sensuous body of a woman but the one who has visualized the essence of love, which lies beyond physical attraction. Shakespeare has brought out this in his play *Romeo and Juliet.* Romeo's friend Mercutio teases him about his previous sweet heart describing her physical charm:

> I conjure thee by Rosaline's bright eyes,
> By her high forehead, and her scarlet lips
> By her fine foot, a straight leg, quivering thigh
> And the demesnes that there adjacent lie. (i, ii)

This is the description of a girl by a person who is clearly not in love but is attracted merely by feminine beauty. Therefore, he refers to the eyes, the lips the thighs etc. But Romeo who is deeply in state of spiritual love for his sweet heart describes Juliet in the following lines:

O! She doth teach the torches o burn bright
It seems she hangs upon the cheek of the night
Like a rich jewel in an Ethiopia's ears
Beauty too rich to use, for earth too dear!

Hemingway's fictional world offers a situation which goes beyond the Shakespearean vision of love in *The Sun Also Rises*. Love between man and woman exists even though they are incapable of deriving sexual pleasures out of the union.

In this manner, Hemingway's artistic vision offers an amazing picture of man-woman relationship where physical attraction is but initial factor. It is love for the suffering humanity. This love develops through continuous struggle, which can be described as labor. Love and Labor thus are invaluable aspects of the Hemingway fiction.

REFERENCES

1. Narayan Sharmah, *Ernest Hemingway: A Critical Study of His Novels With Special Reference to his Treatment to Love* (Thesis). Meerut University, Meerut, October 1974, p. 178.
2. John Killinger, *Hemingway and the Dead Gods: A study in Existentialism*, University of Kentucky Press, 1960, p. 18.
3. *Ibid.*, p. 64.
4. Sulabha Pagey, *Ernest Hemingway: An Introduction of the Themes of His Novels* [Thesis]. Vikram University, Ujjain, April 1974 (Preface).
5. E.H. Rudat Wolfgang, *A Rotten Way to be Wounded: The Tragicomedy of The Sun also Rises.* Peter Lang Publishing INC., NY. 1990, p. 145.
6. *Ibid.*, p. 173.
7. From the Speech by Anders Osterling, Permanent Secretary of the Swedish Academy, at the Presentation Ceremony of the Nobel Prize in 1954, quoted from *American Center Bulletin*, Mumbai, 1999.
8. Kim Moreland, *Hemingway's Medievalist Impulse: Its Effect on the Presentation of Women and War* in the *Sun Also Rises, Hemingway*

Review, Vol. 6. No. 1. Hemingway Society, University of West Florida, Pensacola, Florida, 1986, p. 34.

9. Hannum Howard L., *Jig Jig to Dirty Years, Hemingway Review*; Vol. 11, No. 1. *Fall,* Hemingway Society, University of West Florida, Pensacola, Florida, 1991, p. 46.
10. Michael Culver, *Sparing in the Dark: Hemingway, Strater and the Old Man and the Sea, Hemingway Review*, Vol. 11, No. 2. *Spring,* Hemingway Society, University of West Florida, Pensacola, Florida, 1992, p. 31.
11. Robert Solotaroff, *Sexual Identity in A Farewell to Arms. The Hemingway Review*, Vol. 9. No. 1. *Fall,* Hemingway Society, University of West Florida, Pensacola, Florida, 1989, p. 3.
12. Nirmal, Mukharjee, *Hemingway Woman and Sexual Politics* (*Research Paper*), p. 9.
13. J.D. Dougles (ed.), *New Bible Dictionary. Intervarsity Press, London 1962, p. 753.*

4

OF HUMAN TRAGEDY: HEMINGWAY'S CONCEPT OF TRAGEDY AND ITS DEMONSTRATION THROUGH HIS FICTION

Tragedy is an eminent form of literature. It is a genre which has been dealt with by the eminent classical writers. It somehow came to be associated with poetry in general. This is the reason why Aristotle deals with tragedy in his famous discourse *Poetics*[1] calling it synonymous to poetry. Aristotle's was perhaps the first important discussion of tragedy in a serious and meaningful way. *Poetics* is a kind of retaliation of Plato's famous objection to art and the artist. Plato had argued that artists are dreamers who ideal away the time doing nothing for their society. He termed art as "thrice removed from reality." Aristotle tries to justify the relevance of art to society. He primarily discusses the famous tragedies written by his contemporaries. Therefore, the Aristotelian argument remains confined to tragic plays in Greek, which were at the same time works of high poetry, Aristotle's concept of tragedy has been a source of several other thinkers of the following generations. Aristotle finds the source of tragedy in the character himself. "Character is the destiny" is his famous pronouncement. This Aristotelian tragic hero is a man of highest stature—God or lofty king, prince or princes. This tragic hero has a flaw in his personality, which Aristotle calls *Hamartia*. It is this tragic flaw, which leads him gradually towards the tragic end, in the mean time, several things take place. Several issues are brought in. Revenge, ambition mistaken judgement, thwarted affection bring grief and add to the main action of the story. The tragic hero unknowingly gets involved in all factors and finally dies.

Stoicism is an important trait of the Aristotelian tragic hero. He struggles stoically against the circumstances, which are the creation of his own deeds but which remain beyond his control. Pity and sympathy are the major emotions evoked by tragedy because it essentially becomes the human tragedy with which every mortal being is concerned.

Hegel's concept of human tragedy is based on the conflict of good with good. He cites the example of *Antigone* the famous play by Sophocles in which the protagonist is caught between the domestic responsibilities and those of the state. Hegel has commented while discussing the tragic effect of *Antigone:*

> The world sank into sorrow and grief because it was the end of the state that the individuals and their moral life should be sacrificed to it. The heart of the world was broken and it was all one with the genuineness of spirit, which has arrived at a feeling of tragedy.[2]

Tragedy has been an equally eminent genre during the European renaissance. Writers like Christopher Marlowe and Shakespeare wrote famous tragedies. The Shakespearean tragedy is based largely on the classical rules laid down by Aristotle. However, Shakespeare was romantic in temperament and so too individualist to remain confine to the classical norms in their totality. Therefore, he deviated from the classical roots to some extent. Nevertheless, his concept of tragic hero is more or less similar to that of Aristotle. The Shakespearean tragic hero is a man of high rank. He always suffers from the inner flaw in his personality, which is the cause of tragedy in his life. He gets involved with issues like love, affection, responsibility etc. during the course of action and is led away to tragedy. For Shakespeare as for Aristotle—"character is the destiny."

The concept of tragedy changed considerably in the course of time. The Hegelian concept was that of the romantic philosopher who believed in the revolutionary spirit of an individual and its conflict with the traditional morality. Towards the end of 19th century, high and intense tragedy was possible even in the life of a layman. Thomas Hardy's *Tess* is an ordinary woman yet her stoicism and endurance against the hostile circumstances are as appealing as those of King Oedipus, King Lear, or Hamlet are. By this time man was caught by those factors, which produced the modernist sensibility in the Western society and literature. The entire Western World—both Europe and America—was stirred intellectually and emotionally. The evil of individual revolution and Darwin's theory of evolution laced man within the track of his own creation. Darwin's theory put forth yet another equally important notion of man and his circumstances, namely, *Determinism.*

Darwin had demonstrated that man is no longer a giant striding the earth but a helpless victim of circumstances, which are always beyond his control. Determinism views man as helpless before the outer factors. These factors could be socio-political, economic, and biological and also related with one's race and gender. The pessimism associated with deterministic view of life pervades the work of almost all the modernist writers in Europe as well as in America. It came to be associated with Naturalism, which was a major literacy device adopted and practiced by the late 19th century American novelists. The 20th century American novel discards Naturalism as a literacy device and tends to be more realistic. However, determinism and the pessimism associated with it remained as parts of the artistic vision of the 20th century American novelist.

Hemingway demonstrates the pessimism with the deterministic view of life. His concept of tragedy is formulated by several factors, which were responsible for modernism as a literary concept.

Most of the novels and short stories Ernest Hemingway wrote are tragic. The tragedy in the Hemingway fiction is the result of circumstances often beyond the control of tragic hero.

The body of Hemingway's work becomes one of the most compelling and varied achievements in tragedy that fiction has to offer. He is perhaps the greatest maker of tragedy of the century, considering the range of tragic vision he displays and a variety of characters he creates.

Nick Adams, the protagonist of *In Our Time*, witnesses the infliction of suffering and pain and gets a substantial shock. These stories meet the first test of tragedy and account for young Nick's tragic shock. In some stories he is identified not by the same name and in some stories, not by any name at all. These stories make some discoveries about the nature of life and death that the human society confronts. Eleven stories are the "odyssey of revelation and discovery" of a man from boyhood to maturity. As the boy Nick Adams, the hero, makes certain discoveries about the nature of life and death (*Indian Camp, The Doctor and the Doctor's Wife*). As a late adolescent, still in Michigan, he reinforces and enlarges these discoveries (*The End Of Something, The Three Day Blow, The Battler*). As a young soldier on the Italian Front in World War I, he undergoes the catastrophe of a severe wound and an ill-fated love affair (*A Very Short Story*). After the war, as Krebs in *Soldier's Home,* he is an alien in his own home and country and finds himself no longer suited to either. Returned to Europe with a wife, he discovers in marriage a subtle frustration and sense of loss; in wandering, he feels the vacancy of alienation (Cat *in the Rain, Out of Season, Cross Country Snow*). Finally, having been witnessed to an unending montage of violence, absurdity, and suffering, he returns alone to the Michigan woods (*Big Two Hearted River*).

The first inter-chapter of *In Our Time* points the course of the book; the last serves to summarize it. The first suggests that life is a journey in the dark; the last declares that the great necessity is to survive. Those in between chiefly dramatize the harshness that Hemingway then saw as the core of life, and the inextricability of pleasure and pain. Together, the stories and the inter-chapters reach the following conclusions and affirm the views of life, whether it was reached awarely or intuitively.

These views can be summed up as—(1) violence, brutality, and disappointment are the part of the substance of life. (2) In this harsh universe, pleasure and pain are inter-woven and inseparable. (3) No matter what, life goes on. (4) The first and the final duty is to survive. (5) Man attains his largest stature when he meets the hostile elements with style and control. The world is cruel, purposeless, sometimes ridiculous, and always capricious, life and death occur in it randomly but simultaneously after a fashion; pleasure co-exists with pain—and humor with horror, though the humor is essentially gallows humor. The mass screaming on the pier at midnight suggests that pain and irrationality are the center of the universe; the Turkish officer's delight at the promised punishment of the British sailor dramatizes the fused relationship of pleasure and pain; the fact that the sailor is both innocent and not really to be punished intimates an element of incongruity and ridiculousness in the universe.

In Our Time also portrays woman who refuses to give up newborn babies who have died. This is an example of the closeness of life and death and the irrationality that is part of the life process. An old woman who dies and has instant rigor mortis demonstrates again the omnipresence of death and the universal incongruity (instant rigor mortis is supposed to be impossible). An exchange of gunfire between the narrator's warship and the Turkish shore batteries is barely averted, it would have resulted in a bloodbath, which is another suggestion of incongruous violence always ready to erupt. Emblems of destruction and death are always present; yet joined to those concomitants of death are those of life continuing. Wirt Williams has brought it out very well:

> You didn't mind the women who were having babies as you did those with the dead ones. They had them all right. Surprising how few of them died. You just covered them over with something and let them go to it.
> The harsh portrait of the harsh world is completed in a final image of cruelty, death, and absurdity; the Greeks kill their mules by breaking their legs and pushing them

> into the sea. Thus is sketched the picture of the world that the young man chiefly, known as Nick Adams must confront.... It brings the book full cycle—not only back to Nick but back to the Michigan woods as a paradigm of the universe. It dramatizes Nick's achieved recovery from personal catastrophe to reunion with the life force and a renewal of his own life, and it thus completes his chronicle and is, in a real if unique sense, his and the book's reconciliation to experience that, at the least, has elements of tragedy in it...it is also the emotional nadir of the collection, and the fullest expression of the central component of the tragic view of life; that something in the universe defeats us all. It is the next-to the-last story and the stands in close relation to the last.[3]

Some of the stories of *Men Without Women,* a collection of stories, published in 1927, contain the most impressive writings of tragedy. "The Undefeated," a story demonstrating Aristotelian flaw and catastrophe, is unarguably tragic. Catastrophes are presented variously. Some are single catastrophes, rendered directly there are double catastrophes one character sustains the principal catastrophe, others sustain a shadow catastrophe. Nick sometimes suffers principal catastrophe, and sometimes a shadow of it. Philip Young has edited these stories in a sequential form, a consistent form, under the title *The Nick Adams's Stories.* These stories offer noblest tragic conditions, the fatal flaw. In "The Undefeated" the tragic condition and fatal flaw is associated with aging matador who has also the elevating quality of heroic identity.

Manual Garcia's determination to continue with his art—which he must scan with his life—has brought him nearer and nearer to death. It is mortal flaw and supreme virtue. It is understood, roughly, that the pattern here is an often-repeated one. His absolute determination has won him a shabby fight many times; he has briefly touched artistic fulfillment with brilliant performance right up to the inevitable disaster—the killing of the bull—then his shortcoming with the sword both destroys his previous excellence in the *faena* and brings him injury. In each bull fighting, the kill is his immediate catastrophe; his inability to kill well constitutes a lesser, but equally fatal, flaw.

Like *The Old Man and the Sea,* "The Undefeated" intersects other sub-species of tragedy. Manuel suffers from a Heilmanic division of essences; the confrontation between the dictates of common sense to give up fighting and of his passion to continue it produces the fateful, but ennobling and transcending choice. Also, there is an element of Hegelian tragedy here, for Manuel represents a 'good' imperative to be sensible and give it up—may seem at first to have no adequate objectification. But if one looks closely he finds that Zurito, the picador, fits splendidly. Zurito helps Manolo, on the condition the Manuel will retire if he fails. At the end, the scene between the two thus emerges as the final confrontation between the two imperatives. Zurito is trying to cut his pigtail, the mark of the matador; gravely wounded, Manuel stops him. The imperative of the passion prevails, and it will very shortly carry Manuel to his death. More powerfully than any earlier story, this one dramatizes the famous Hemingway 'double-dicho,' a philosophic aphorism that means almost the same if reversed; 'A man may be destroyed but not defeated.' Hence, the title *The Undefeated.*

In *A Canary for One,* there is a death of love when the marriage ends. *In Hills Like White Elephants,* man persuades his beloved to have an abortion; killing their love and denying their own possibility. In *Ten Indians,* also similarly the love is lost. *Banal Story* is flooded with confrontation of death of Maera, the matador. In *Another Country* a cheerful Italian major collapses emotionally at the news of his wife's sudden death, and thinks that the end of romantic love is death and that any promises of happiness the universe makes, are false. *A Pursuit Race* shows efforts of a bicycle rider who loses race against the man who starts behind him. He feels catastrophe like a man defeated in the bed. *The Killers* produced tragedy the impact of which is observed on the witness. Gangsters appear at the dinner, tie up Nick and a co-worker, and calmly prepare the murder of Ole Anderson without warning. This, to Nick, appears almost taken his life and then released unharmed. But when he goes to warn the primary he finds that Ole Andreson has decided to accept death without further resistance. He must die without a mysterious transgression. Nick is forced to understand that there is evil in the universe that cannot be explained, conquered, or evaded. In *An Alpine Idyll,* life and death are juxtaposed and there is an end of love. The narrator hears the unnatural heat of the mountain sun as an attempt to flee the life force but can not escape from their secondhand encounter with the peasant Olz, who mutilates his wife's body by hanging a lantern from the open mouth of her frozen corpse and reduces her to the level of inanimate convenience, a woman he loved. It was a brutality latent in romantic love. In *Fifty Grand* victory is defeat and defeat victory and the catastrophe is so problematic to know as to which is which. Jake Brennan bets fifty thousand dollars against himself in a title defense, he has inverted the apparent scheme of things; to win, he has to lose. Jake's real enemy is time, not his opponent and it is from time that he wishes to wrest the psychic transcendent victory. The unanticipated ordeal that Jake must survive to make his wish to come true emphasizes the irony of his triumph-in-loss. In *A Simple Enquiry* the Italian major's intention brings catastrophe without signal and almost simultaneously when he delicately makes a homosexual advance towards his orderly. *After the Storm,* asserts that life promises and then takes away: all life forms ultimately prey upon and consumes one another. The savage fight between captain of the boat and a stranger is reasonless here. The captain's fight comes upon the false understanding of the man who has died. His character as scavenger and predator is revealed by the attempt to loot an abandoned schooner, and what he finally finds is the result of a large, more capricious violence by nature, the big liner is grounded in quicksand just under water. The random violence and absurdity have created a steam of greed and gratification. Whatever he can take from a dead vessel belongs to him by the law of savage. But others have already taken booty. Teasing universe has promised him everything but left him with nothing. The captain ends in catastrophe. *The*

Sea Change is a classic form; a young woman discloses to her love that she is going away for a lesbian affair by which he is hurt. But he forgives her and sends her off with his blessings. Human beings break out of self-isolation to join humanity. The young man comes out of the catastrophe of his shattered self-enclosed pride to attain compassion and community. In *Homage to Switzerland,* the three Americans pause for meal at the railroad cafes; snow falling outside affects them. This suggests that destructive force of hostile universe is indifferent to the common man. The cafe becomes a refuge but does not work by itself. Sufferers are ultimately alone and confront pain catastrophe alone. Life is a cheat, and man must suffer. This is what Ernest Hemingway believed in, which he has revealed in the *God Rest You Merry, Gentlemen.* In *Wine of Wyoming,* Fontana feels himself a victim of catastrophe. He is fallen in his own eyes tragically when his desperate attempts fail to get wine for a communion ritual to offer to his friends. *A Clean Well-Lighted Place* is built upon twin catastrophes. The old man attempts suicide the week before as the two waiters watch him drinking in the sidewalk café. The one waiter feels sympathy for the old man because he also confronts Nada and hopelessness. This is man's eternal confrontation with the void.

Hemingway's stories are invariably tragic. *Capital of the World* is the story of Paco's indiscrimination romanticism, an impulse to be a bull fighter. This impulse prompts him to accept challenge from Enrique, the dishwasher who emulates bull by heavy sharp knives to the legs of a chair. Paco's death comes directly to him from his desire to prove truly brave in his own eyes. It is the noble youthful aspiration and fatal flaw that surrounds and brings death through the risky game.

Francis Macomber, in *The Short Happy Life of Francis Macomber* climbs out of that disgrace to triumph and get destroyed. There is redemptive effect of course in his death. He comes closest to accepting death deliberately for his new vision. His wife's contemptuous betrayal of the hunter Wilson brings nadir of his self esteem. The recovery of physical wound and the subsequent translation of it into the strength to overthrow his wife make Macomber feel face the buffalo and kill it. What he does for is comparative a small thing, a masculine assertion.

> The car was going a wild forty-five miles an hour across the open, and as Macomber watched, the buffalo got bigger and bigger until he could see the gray, hairless, scabby look of one huge bull and how his neck was a part of his shoulders and the shiny black of his horns as he galloped a little behind the others that were strung out in that steady plunging gait...they drew up close and he could see the plunging hugeness of the bull, and the dust in his sparsely haired hide, the wide boss of horn and his outstretched, wide-nostriled in...and the car skidded, plowing sideways to an almost stop and Wilson was out on one side and he on the other stumbling as his feet hit the still speeding by of the earth, and then he was shooting at the bull as he moved away, hearing the bullets whunk into him.[4]

The truth lies in the instant of time, which is not compellingly presented here or in any other single passage of the story. The truth is in the whole: that man should be ready to pay price to enter his full potential and identity. This has always been the perception of some of the great tragedies

Hemingway has evolved in *The Snow of Killimanjaro* even greater intensification of Greek tragedy. The last scene of the last act of the story is full of intensity, shattering, emotional impact. Harry, the protagonist, is brought down by fate, which attributes much of the powers of Shakespearean tragedy, where Harry surrenders his talent for comfort, marries the rich woman, and betrays his self. His attempt to come out of corruption, achieve wholesome life, and rise again is his great intention, which culminates in death. Harry's attempt is the attempt of doom. He is doomed by the accidental thorn scratch, which he does not treat. As a result blood poisoning is caused and Harry contracts gangrene, which finally kills him. His own flaw and the hostile unknown in the universe together have destroyed him. He is caught between his need and compulsion between which he struggles. Death is a kind of reconciliation between the two. His relinquishment of work and personal negation followed thereof, destroyed him. His own weakness was the cause of his moral disintegration and incongruous, carelessness, gratuitous acts against the moral universe.

> And now this life...was coming to a term because he had not used iodine two weeks ago when a thorn had scratched his knee as they moved forward trying to photograph a herd of water duck standing.[5] Harry's neglect of it is the working of his own flaw, his destructive force. It is a genuine Poundian image, for it projects the substance of all Harry's life: the drive to create, the failure, the fate-inflicted damage that is made lethal by his own destructive carelessness.... The infection of the flesh is a metaphor of Harry's infection of the spirit. and it has brought him to the threshold of death as the story formally begins.[6] Even brutal declaration of what is to come, Harry says on the cot, 'the marvelous thing is that it's painless. An instant visualization of waiting vultures, perhaps more frightening for being named only as birds.[7]

Life is tragic according to Hemingway. The real triumph of life is possible only in death but the quest for life must go on.

There are two main factors, which make *The Sun Also Rises* essentially a tragedy: (1) The protagonist suffers catastrophe, which is irreversible on its own term and (2) the work should have sufficient powerful impact. *The Sun also Rises* satisfies both the tests. Therefore, it is a powerful tragedy according to him. It is parallel to Greek Tragedy.

Jake Barnes, after receiving the war wounds finds himself incapable of conventional sexual expression and is simply trying to come to terms with life. There he becomes successful to a greater extent but when Brett Ashley re-enters his life, he surrenders to emotions her returns evokes. This knocks down what he had achieved and enters catastrophe. This novel is far closer to Frye's omnipotence of the crushing-universe boundary of tragedy. Jake is overwhelmed by circumstances. His, falling in love with Brett, though involuntary to take more from life than it has left him. This has set in motion his catastrophe. In the words of Wirt Williams:

> Jake's wound is the consequence of his flying in the Italian air arm, and it was patently a romanticism, a thrust toward the ineluctable, that caused him to enlist in a foreign force in the first place. So his romanticism both caused his wound and caused him to fall in love with Brett. This was the fatal flaw, which causes Jake to sustain catastrophe both because, of the operational hostility of the universe and because of a quality in himself.[8]

Jake reaches his personal nadir when he debases himself in his own eyes by handing Brett to the bullfighter and takes a humiliating beating from his philosophical and tonal antagonist, Robert. Man is finally helpless before the dictate of an indifferent but punishing universe; he can only dignify himself by the manner in which he accepts the inescapable catastrophe.

In *The Sun Also Rises,* all characters suffer a loss and pain of overpowering universe in traumatic proportions. This was a kind of moral examination of them. Robert Cohn is another character who suffers; humiliated in marriage, he sought to regain his self-esteem in the relationship with Frances but found to be trapped and becomes infatuated with Brett to spend a weekend with her. He thinks he has achieved what he wanted but falls from that pinnacle into catastrophe when he sees the woman he loves, in the arms of other man Mike Campbell, another male character, also suffers. His bankruptcy in business is presented as a concomitance of a personal bankruptcy. He somehow makes friendship with Brett to fall from his unsafe perch.

Brett also suffers in the same manner. The death of her lover and two destructive marriages have reduced her to promiscuity. She has pulled herself upward to brief self-respect by her love for Jake, but is pushed off by the tension created by Jake's impotency. Her weekend with Robert makes her return by choice to her old ways but her catastrophe had already begun with the agonies of her unfulfilled love for Jake. The catastrophe is created by her self-loathing, until she reconciles herself with young matador. When Jake steps on the cockroach in the Bayonne hotel lobby, one inevitably thinks of that insets are to man as man are to a higher power. The earl of Gloucester in *King Lear* has pronounced it well:

> As flies to wanton boys are we to the Gods
> They kill us for their sports (4.I, 36-37).

One way out of the universal catastrophe is communion in formal religion. Jake and Brett try to achieve this communion. Jake does not discount religion but only presents for it inadequately in the cathedral. He says:

> ...regret I was such a rotten Catholic, but realized there was nothing I could do about it, at least for a while and maybe never, but that anyway it was a grand religion (97),[9] Brett says later, God never worked very well with me.[10]

In Pamplona, at the fiesta, the only gods are the bulls. The worship of the bull-god at the *corrida* is a celebration of the tragic act wherein the man and the bull both die. This is a inescapable and the ultimate truth. Everything is mortal. Nothing is living. Yet in the face of death, both the bull and the man maintain their dignity. But the death is ultimate in the prayer of universe. Jake faces the catastrophe by accepting it with grace and dignity and responsibility and devotes himself to the reward of consolation that is available. "You like to eat, don't you? Jake replies that he likes to do a lot of things" (246) ..."Oh, Jake," Brett said, "we could have had such a damn good time together." Ahead was a mounted policeman in traffic. He raised his baton. The car slowed suddenly pressing Brett against me. "Yes," I said. "Isn't it pretty to think so?"[11]

Thus, Hemingway has placed the characters in *The Sun Also Rises* near the absolute boundary of tragedy, the concept that man is inevitable destroyed by the forces of universe, which is hostile. In Hegel's tragedy of the collision of conflicting essences, the opposing elements are inescapable death and a will to take a kind of victory from that death. Heilman's tragedy proceeds from a fateful choice between two fundamental possibilities, in that perspective, Cantwell chooses to make an arduous expedition and to make love to his woman, knowing that his choice for happiness will precipitate his death. It will be remembered that there are two philosophic definitions, or boundaries of the tragic field. One holds that tragedy demonstrated the omnipotence of the universe at the expense of the individual; the other says that something within man himself is always the most active agent of his destruction. Like most of Hemingway's protagonists, Cantwell is undone by the inimical cosmos. But his stubborn insistence on finishing life according to his own design makes a substantial contribution to his tragedy. Finally, both the hero and story exist between tragic limits and touch both.

A Farewell to Arms of Ernest Hemingway is the greatest tragedy of romantic love. The love of a couple takes initiation at the backdrop of massive war. Baker calls it the first study in doom. This novel foreshadows the consequences of devastations caused by war to the humanity. This has been described by Ernest Hemingway in his earlier novel *The Sun Also Rises,* as stated above. The happiness of humanity is withdrawn and destroyed by the armed forces. Consequently, the semi-pastoral life of Frederic Henry in Gorizia is disintegrated by the advent of real war. The consummation of love between Frederic Henry and Catherine Barkley appears to be a reprieve from war, but only temporarily. The doom constantly threatens them as war continues. The war in the dark is like a summer lightening. The lovers struggle for the ultimate good, dimly aware of the hostile universe thrusting war upon them. War, therefore, becomes their enemy. Catherine's pregnancy is sure to bring disaster. There is no escape to both of them. This war is going to shape their fate. Doom of physical life of Catherine and annihilation of emotional life of Henry is going to follow soon. Before meeting Catherine, Henry was advised by his priest friend to go and visit Abruzzi a worth visiting place during the holidays, where the peaceful life exists with peaceful people. Henry does not follow this advice. Instead, he drifts in the plain, the cities for gratification and roams about in bars and whorehouses. This indicated that he was advancing towards a different destiny sure to doom. In Catherine, he found his happy home but the fear still lurked from which there is no escape as he is within the outreach of enemy. Love of the couple brings them finally to the point of tragedy from where there is no return. Plain, rain, fog and snow contribute to the agony of the couple. The highest mountain of peace and happy life to which they intend to reach becomes invisible because of fog and rain. War impedes in their fulfillment.

Doom continues to shadow their hope. Henry and Catherine approach a cathedral, which is sanctuary for other lovers; they pass and leave it behind in rain-mist. One of the most forceful and sadly ironic of all such images is that of the umbrella; as they escape by boat to Switzerland, they try to use the umbrella to catch the wind. They speed ahead, then it buckles and collapses. 'I was astride the handle of an inside-out, ripped umbrella where I had been holding a wind-filled pulling sail' (290). Wirt Williams puts it better:

> A positive force—their love—is in one instant transported into ruin and futility; such concentrated forewarnings never let us forget the inevitability of catastrophe and keep the tragic spirit of the novel ever in our consciousness."[12]

The universe is the hostile force to the lovers. War contributes to make tragedy worst of its kind. Catherine while driven away in the carriage leans-out and points at the carabinieri (military policeman), which is a metaphorical warning of catastrophe to come. In addition, when their car stops at the old headquarters at Gorizia Henry lies in Rinaldi's bed, while it rained outside, concomitantly *nada* follows.

All the disasters of the retreat take place in the rain; the killing of Aymo by his own troops, the arrest of Henry, the execution of other officers. The rain continues as Henry escapes by his neobaptismal plunge into the river and continues even after he finds a shaky sanctuary in the guns under the canvas of a flatcar. It is falling even when he rejoins Catherine in bed in

Tresa, and when the barman brings news of Henry's impending arrest he is dripping from the rain. The rain becomes spasmodic as Catherine and Henry begin their escape by boat and halts as they reach a safe part of the lake and safely. A fine, 'falsely cheerful' rain greets them in Switzerland.

It stops completely as they enter the high good country of the mountains and is not to begin again until they must descend to the plain for what will be Catherine's death. It precisely marks the end of fulfillment. Later, in the hospital, it begins as Catherine is wheeled into the operating theater for a cesarean and, therefore, envelops all the action until her death. Then in the final image, Henry walks back to the hotel in the rain is more systematic and sustained than other images. Nevertheless, the plain is the place of all disasters—though also the beginning of the love affair. In addition, war images—soldiers, guns, gunfire, vehicle shuttle constantly through the books, assuming more and more configuration. The rain ultimately joins the death.

Carlos Baker brings out the point effectively:

> Any one who reads *A Farewell to Arms* with one eye on the weather will eventually marvel as he watches the another playing with falling rain as a symbol of imminent doom. Near the close of the book when Catherine is approaching her time of confinement the weather warm and the rains arrives. For a whole miraculous winter the lovers have gloried in their isolation, living happily in their high mountain fastness, surrounded by healthy cold air and clean snow, far from the mud and muck of war. Now at last the rains come, the time for the dying-in draws near, some great change lurks beyond the lovers' limited horizon, and we begin to sense that Catherine is in mortal danger, as indeed, she is.[13]

Henry's recollection of ants on the end of a fog in a campfire, recalls the lines from *King Lear.* He idly throws water on the log but it steams, rather than aids the ants, and he makes no move to save them. The often—perceived implication:

the power in the universe is the dog searching a garbage can vainly; Henry tells him. 'There isn't anything, dog' (315). Much earlier comes an almost humorous refraction of the theme in the comments of the British major at the officers' club in Milan; He said we were all cooked, but we were all right as long as we did not know it. We were all cooked. The thing was not to recognize it... It was all balls... They all squabbled about divisions and only killed them when they got them.... We were all cooked.... 'Good-by,' he said, then cheerily, 'Every sort of luck'. There was a great contrast between his world pessimism and personal cheeriness (133-34). Thus, the tragedy is shaped. Frederic and Catherine confront a hostile universe, and fight it for their happiness.

Finally, there comes the dominance of *nada,* which destroys man and the man is helpless before it. When Catherine dies Henry experiences full force of catastrophe. His entire commitment to romantic love brings catastrophe to him. Pleasure of love results into the pain of Catherine's death. The fire that warms Henry destroys ants. Thus, *A Farewell to Arms* is one of purest tragedies that Ernest Hemingway crafted. *A Farewell to Arms* thus, becomes one of the greatest novels of modern times.

To Have and Have Not, is yet another tragic novel. It is written with the intention to expose disparity and malfunctioning of American society of his time. It is the Aristotelian tragedy of fatal flaw, located somewhere between Frye's concept of tragedy arising out of: (1) Powerlessness of individual against universe and (2) falling through protagonist's own failure. Man participates in shaping his own catastrophe. There is, therefore, a sharing of responsibility for the catastrophe. In this novel, the catastrophe of Harry Morgan's life begins with the opening of the novel; its culmination is in his death. Hostile forces draw steadily around him. His determination that he will maintain his self-sufficiency at all cost and the illusion that he can control his own destiny bring the catastrophe. He has been forced to go for illegal means of earning his living, which he did not intend to. But the world deprived him of right to make a reasonable living on his own reasonable terms. He is a victim of tragic necessity and of a failed economic system of America. He pursues his own fatal flaw and murders two individuals who were murderers themselves and who were committed to living their lives on their own terms and imposing their terms on the universe. Hemingway seems to emphasis that those, who try to conquer alone, die alone. But, of course, all die alone, no matter how small or ruthless he or she is.

Harry Morgan is doomed in his struggle with the universe by the nature of things, but to a more significant degree he is the engineer of his own catastrophe by his mistaken apprehension of reality, he seems fated to catastrophe at the hands of tragic necessity, but he fights back in pride and isolation. His pride becomes *hubris;* his belief that he can survive alone, and even triumph alone, is a misunderstanding that ultimately kills him and precipitates catastrophe as finality. Harry is battered not only by the ineluctable, but also by things as they are, politically and economically, in the United States during the depression; his first betrayer is the businessman, his second, a government official. The novel consequently becomes a political statement, if an emotional one, as well as formal tragedy. The book begins like a Greek tragedy, with the first perceptible movement towards catastrophe in the life of the protagonist. *Oedipus Rex* begins at the final phase of the whole myth; so with Harry. He is first encountered at the highest point he is to reach in terms of his most profound desire or intention; he has achieved a boat and a family and is supporting the second with the first honestly and fairly. He is living on his own terms but the struggle to reach this personal pinnacle can only be deduced, and the novel halted. It starts from a betrayal of Harry by an American businessman; it ends with Harry dying on the deck of another man's boat.

Although Harry survives and the Chinese adventure, the forces operating against him, intensify. The Depression keeps Harry from earning a living by chartering his boat for fishing and his choice to act outside the law rather than succumb, lose the boat, and go on relief is a Heilmanic, tragedy—developing choice. Hauling liquor, he is wounded by the Coast Guard;

because of freakish bad luck—a high Federal official on a fishing trip sees him wounded and reports him—his boat is impounded and he loses the arm. Still holding stubbornly to his choice, he accepts the most dangerous job he has ever undertaken, that of carrying revolutionaries back to Cuba after they have robbed a Key West bank; he must rent a boat himself to do it. His plan to kill all of them before they kill him is the final manifestation of his *hubris,* and though it almost succeeds, it ends with Harry gasping his life out on the deck. Awareness has apparently come. He has learnt something, at least, of the nature of the forces, which have oppressed him; nothing can beat them and it was his fatal error to think he could. In his fall, the working of fate and his own character have been inextricable interlocked:

> As they turned out of the door to the right, I saw a closed car across the square towards them. The first thing a pane of glass went and the bullet smashed into the row of bottles on the showcase wall to the right. I heard the gun gong and bop, bop, bop there were bottles smashing along the wall (6).

Order is shattered without warning by violence lying beneath the deceptively tranquil surface of life. Both the orders of Harry's life and his life itself are to be shattered by the same violence, and further irony, by Cuban. Harry is sad and reflective after the young men approached him. And his regret at the death, showing clearly the deep changes in his character that have been wrought in the interval. Harry's concept of himself as his own ultimate authority is instantly apparent when his messenger brings him word of the fight of Mr. Johnson, with the $ 825 due to Harry. He accepts the responsibility of the loss and the responsibility for making it good, by any means. Here he does not blame fate but himself; he sends Frankie, the dock bum, out to find him profitable contraband to haul. It never occurs to him to abandon his responsibility, surrender his self-sufficiency, and return home defeated to starve or go on relief—not to turn elsewhere. But he knows he has taken a decisive turn and is filled with foreboding, a foreboding that is instantly justified when Frankie comes in with Mr. Sing. Harry is ruthless in assessing the situation and planning the action, he considers he must take to preserve himself, but even then, some compassion enters his decision and he transforms into Aristotle's tragic protagonist who is neither all good nor all bad. He makes the commander's decision to save the most at the expense of the fewest; instead of killing the contraband Chinese as Mr. Sing delicately suggests, he kills Mr. Sing instead, breaking the entrepreneur's neck on the boat while receiving payment. Later, Eddie asks him why, and he answers, 'to keep from killing twelve other Chinks' (5). The same space in his ruthlessness is revealed when he spares Eddie.

After Beelips tells Harry his Coast guard is found and repossessed his stolen boat, he embodies another fatal quality for Harry, becoming messenger and manifestation of the destructive element in the universe; because he is himself so clearly marked as its victims, he becomes its emblem. Harry viscerally identified him that way as he warns him, 'keep your mouth off my business...you're poison to any one whoever touched you' (122). Harry knows Beelips will be smashed because he has stupidly set in motion forces he does not understand.

Is this unpredictable bad luck or inevitable and inescapable concomitant of his action? The question is not a real one; from the beginning, it was a *probability* that Harry would be killed in a fight with four armed men. His *hubris* has assaulted logic as well as tragic necessity, and he has come to his logical, foreseeable end. Has he also come to awareness? Dying, he considers, 'I guess it was nuts all right. I guess I bit off to much more than I could chew.' But he does not wish to relinquish his conviction that he really had no choice: 'Hell, I couldn't run no filling station.' Awareness comes, if it comes, with his dying speech to the Coast Guard petty officers who board the boat: 'A man,' Harry Morgan said 'one man alone ain't got no bloody fucking chance.' He shut his eyes. It had taken him a long time to get time to get it out and it had taken him all of his life to learn it.

Is this a primitive, intuitive revolutionary declaration? Or a postulation of a primitive, intuitive tragic sense of life? Or both? The important thing is that Harry is not in the least a thinking man but a feeling one. He *feels* the world against him; he is deeply, emotionally aware of that operational hostility with its abstract indifference. He is convinced now the universe crushes the individual. Something, which demonstrates the pitiless power of the universe in its confrontation with the individual. But for Harry, as for many men, this confrontation *appears* to be an economic one. He has been forced, he considers, into his choices and his actions because the world has deprived him of the right to make a reasonable living on his own reasonable terms. His resentment is profound and total but is directed at the life itself. Indeed, Harry is the victim of tragic necessity and of a failed economic system; his last declaration is the cry of both tragic protagonist and belated revolutionary. In these specifics, certainly, Harry has come to awareness. Has he come to awareness in another major dimension—that of perceiving and acknowledging his own fatal flaws, of character and of action? His admission, 'I guess it was nuts.... I shouldn't have tried it,' balances with his feeling that he couldn't have done anything else. Like most protagonists of tragedy, Harry touches both, its limits: he has been crushed by the universe in the nature of things, and his own character and acts have precipitated his catastrophe. But one feels in leaving him that his acknowledgment of responsibility is not complete—that finally he sees himself as undone by overwhelming mysterious powers and refuses to accept fully his own flaw as an equal cause. He has come to awareness—but it is not total. Nor has he truly transcended his catastrophe: he has won no absolute psychic victory in his physical defeat, other than demonstrating physical courage, which is final and unredeemed. He is genuine tragic protagonist, though not of the highest and noblest order.

For Whom the Bell Tolls, offers an epic variety of experience. Baker calls it a tragic epic. The book is engaged with the great political events and issues of the time in Spanish Republic. In this novel Hemingway emphasizes the brutalities of Fascist government of Spain and sympathies for the communists. Showing their spots and virtues Hemingway points out that Communism and Republicanism are not the same, rather they are co-belligerents. The novel contains several varieties of tragedy of personal flaw that dignifies and ennobles but then destroys the character and finally Hemingway's own tragedy in which protagonists co-author their own catastrophe.

Robert Jordan, the protagonist, undertakes his mission to blow up the bridge for Golz, develops the incarnation of an ethical absolute—duty to cause, and duty to one's immediate group, the band with which he is working for the mission. Maria, a female protagonist, raped by fascist, becomes the embodiment of another absolute. The romantic love that Maria and Jordan make is a to all commitment to each other in the four days that are available to them. Maria makes Jordan aware of his duty, as a result, there is confrontation between love and duty within him. Bridge becomes the concentration of all forces: military forces of enemy, destructive and absurd forces of nature, fascism, the force of negative human liberty and dignity, Jordan blows the bridge and is killed in the process. Jordan makes decision of blowing bridge that is fatal and will bring death in all probabilities. He could have easily abandoned the assignment and escaped with Maria. But he does not do so, though there was a choice for him. The Drydenesque heroic tragedy also operates here, which is the tragedy of choice between the two imperatives. There is a choice of two imperative decisions before Jordan, the romantic love of Maria, and the blowing the bridge. He chooses the later *i.e.* blowing of bridge. This brings catastrophe to him; his leg is broken when hit in the action; he does not run away from the field, remains very much on the scene and delays the pursuers by machine gun so that his other people of the band could flee. The assessment of Jordan's decision in Aristotelian terms, is the 'flaw,' ethical—absolute that is fatal, ennobling and self-defining virtue, which brings catastrophe to him. It is the spiritual triumph over material disaster. Jordan affirms:

> I have fought for what I have believed in for a year now. If we win here, we will win every where. The

> world is a fine place and worth the fighting for and I hate very much to; leave it. And you had a lot of luck, he told himself, to have such a good life.... You've had as good a life as any one because of these last days.... I wish there was some way to passion what I've learned ...I'd like to talk to Karkov. That is in Madrid. Just over the hills there, and down across the plain. Down out of the gray rocks and the pines, the heather and gorse, across the yellow high plateau you see rising white and beautiful. That part is just as true as Pilar's old women drinking the blood down at the slaughterhouses. There's no one thing that is true. Thus, he accepts a total order as well as the sum of the events that are his own life. Concomitantly, he appears to understand and accept the working of tragic necessity inside the order. The pervasive idea that war is the expression of the universe's destructive element has found crystallization earlier, immediately after Jordan's leg has been broken. He says that many such things happen in war, and Augustin answers that war is a "bitchery" (501).

The transcendence is reinforcing when Jordan rejects possibility of suicide not only to terminate pain but also to avoid torture and inevitable disclosure of information it will bring. He endures to engage in a fight with the pursuing fascist cavalry that can only end his life but would give his people time. For Hemingway, life is tragic. One defines oneself by the action he takes against catastrophe. *For Whom the Bell Tolls* is chiefly preoccupied with the obligation to the community. All men share a common unity and identity despite their different identities.

The supporting concept that bears most heavily upon the tragic assertion has to do with what men owe one another. They owe everything including their lives and man's chief duty is to do everything he can do for collective human dignity and freedom. The definitive act in the face of catastrophe should be an act in behalf of the human commonalty; it is the individual's chief obligation to sacrifice himself for the human community and his greatest opportunity for a transcendent act.

All humanity has its bright promise and terrifying capacity for acts of darkness. Some get pleasure from inflicting pain on others. Fascists laugh as they abuse and rape Maria. The desire to inflict pain becomes a concomitant of evil in man. Pilar, the other protagonist, adds: "that was the worst day of my life until one other day...three days later when the fascists took the town" (142). The preparation at the hill top sounded in dialogue: "Wipe the pap of your mother's breasts off thy lips...no one of us will see the sun go down this night" (333). The Republicans' efforts to hold to life, which lores the fascist captain to his death—and in the consciousness of El Sordo:

> ...but living was a field of grain blowing in the wind on the side of a hill. Living was a hawk in the sky. Living was an earthen jar of water in the dust of the threshing...living was a horse between your legs and carbine under one leg and a hill and a valley with a stream with trees along it and the far side of the valley and the hills beyond (336).

Across the River and into the Trees is Hemingway's different tragedy. It is a tragedy of individual being overpowered by hostile and uncaring, omnipotent cosmos. Aging Cantwell, a protagonist, in the novel is a retired colonel. He wishes to possess his youth in the form of his beloved Renata, a young shining girl. He is given her to possess, a few days Just before his death. Renata, in the precinct of youth gives Cantwell the happiness he desires. Cantwell knows well that he cannot keep the treasure of union with the past *i.e.,* human continuity, and romantic love as he is aging now. In terms of Aristotle's fatal flaw, Cantwell commits a fatal flaw. His flaw is the desire for the possession of love with bright youthful—Renata. In Hegel's terms there is collision of conflicting essences—inescapable death and victory over death. In Heilman's sense there is choice between two fundamental possibilities: making arduous expedition and making love to Renata. He knows his choice will precipitate death. As has been inherent in the philosophic concept of tragedy there are two components of tragedy: (1) tragedy demonstrates omnipresence of the universe at the expense of the individual and

(2) that something within man himself always is the most active agent of his destruction.

Cantwell's own stubborn insistence of the expedition for fishing is substantial contribution to his tragedy as he is old man and can not sustain the stoic expedition.

Hemingway's central is that life is shaped chiefly by an abstractly indifferent but operationally hostile fate. Man cannot prevent his universal catastrophe; he can control it with bravery and style. In the novel, Cantwell knows that only true happiness of the life—his love for Renata—will be terminated shortly by his damaged heart. He chooses to compress the rest of this life into a last visit to her in Venice and into a duck hunt with his friend Alvarito. The meeting with Renata is his ultimate realization of, and farewell to, romantic love and life. The hunt becomes a final metaphor of his quest for form and beauty as well as a symbolic enactment of his meeting with death. His biological death is almost a postscript to an event already emotional and artistically completed. Though that precedent ritual he has faced the enemies of spirit incarnate in the flesh, has defeated all of them by uncompromising resolution and so has met death on his own terms. This simple scheme of tragedy is profoundly intensified by the fable that underlies it. Renata, the young countess, is the image of the colonel's own youth, and is given to him to possess it again just before death (Renata, means reborn). The portrait of herself that she gives him in his memory of the happiness of his youth. Her family emeralds—which she tries to give him outright but which he knows he cannot keep—are the treasures of union with the past human continuity and romantic love. He dies in perfect reconciliation with such gifts.

Cantwell's attempt to take the duck—to achieve his life's final possibility—is repeatedly impeded by the "big brute" of a pole man of what is ultimately revealed to be a black boat (recoiling the black gondola in another work about death in Venice). In the face of his constant and threatening hostility, the shooter resolutely maintains his determination to achieve a deliberate and final fulfillment. Their duel, too, is conducted against the backdrop of mountains, always the eternal and, absolute. As the shooter helps his boatman, he reflects that they are two third of the way to where they are going; Cantwell is doing his part to go to death properly, with his own strength. Thus the primal conflict is established and particularized in a smaller and an easier one to perceive. So, too, is the line of action defined; a doomed protagonist, moving consciously towards death, fights against powerful opposition to give the last moment, life form and beauty. Tragedy is in visible motion, even if its whole shape is not yet clear. The shooter is revealed as a fifty-year old colonel in the United States Army with a dangerous heart condition, preparing to go to Venice to see his young mistress and, with a friend, to shoot duck. Colonel begins the trip from the army installation at Trieste. As he is driven to Venice in his Buick, he perceives countering images of life and death. They are simultaneous in the colonel's consciousness, bombed buildings, and repairs on a bridge being visible in the same instant. He remembers how he defecated a week before on the exact spot where he had been wounded thirty years before that, how he made a 'monument' by adding to it the amount of money his Italian decorations had produced; home and opposing keys softly resume their contention. The 'monument' underlies the fusion of his personal mortality with the idea of life's continuity: 'It has merge, money, blood, look how that grass grows; and the iron's in the earth along with Gino's leg, both of Randolfo's legs, and my right kneecap.' He remembers the dad in the canals in the first war, bloated and swollen. These are shortly countered by what appears to be life images: a big red sail moving across the land in a canal evokes the colonel's vision of 'the great, slow, pale oxen,' 'a fine,' big mule,' and 'a wolf, gaited like no other animal.' All of these 'move (his) heart' [24].

The first, boat the colonel takes is a metaphor for himself: it is an excellent, well-kept craft with a motor which, like his heart, is failing. His promise to the old owner to get him a replacement engine is not, to be fulfilled, any more than he himself is to get new heart.

The two keys alternate quickly as he passes in the boat under a series of bridges. Interpretation of most of these must be speculative: perhaps the first white bridge connotes his youth; the red bridge, romantic love for Renata; the 'high-flying white bridge', his youth re-grasped; the black bridge that follows, his death. Such sublimation images accumulate, intensifying the tragic tone. He reflects that two stakes in the canal, joined by chains but not in contact, are 'like us' bound together but still apart. In the boat he passes a black diesel craft full of lumber for firewood and later he looks through the window of the Gritty bar at 'the big black hitching post for the gondolas (Boat) and the late afternoon winter light on the windswept water.' Simultaneously, a large black barge coming up the canal is making a steady advance of death. He is already in the trap of tragedy as at this stage Renata enters. Immediately she is defined, subtly but directly, by the words that signify her representational quality—'shining youth.' She wears a funeral black sweater. So she is the colonel's youth, enclosed in his approaching death. The not excessive Christ like character of Cantwell underlies the concept that he is Christ only as all men are Christ: they are born to be crucified and to triumph, if they can, within that crucifixion Cantwell thus merges with youth and love in the black envelope of death. A final exchange of words between the two would make the point clear:

> We should not make love, I know, (says, Renata).
> 'I don't know. Who says it?'
> 'I say it because I love you.... Do you think we could once more if it would not hurt you?'
> 'Hurt me?' The Colonel said. 'When the hell was I ever hurt?' (157).

Their conversation and their movements through Venice contain much that is purely harmonic in character—the physical details of the city and its places, the colonel's reflections on military life—in short, all non-thematic detail. But when he calls her 'Daughter' and asks if she would like to run for 'Queen of Heavens', something important is intended. Cantwell, who often invokes Dante, insinuates here that she is Beatrice, a spiritual constant and support if not guide in his strange journey. That journey, already in one perspective, a return to the past, is soon to become a stepping into the future. After they have parted and he is alone in the hotel room, he places her emeralds 'cold and yet warm, as they moved... from his bad hand into his good hand.' In the pocket of his pajamas, over his heart they become that great Hemingway constant, consolation in catastrophe... The boatmen, death's emissary, continues to mar Cantwell's hunt. Yet in spite of him, the colonel kills a mating pair of ducks, which again evokes the wedding of spirit he has achieved with Renata and it's ending by imminent death—an instant and total illumination. He reflects, 'it is murder. And what, isn't nowadays?'[14]

The Old Man And The Sea is Hemingway's realistic and Christian tragedy. Philip Young called it a triumph of classic tragedy; perhaps the most complex form, and other fables built upon it are equally tragic.[15] It intersects many species and variations of tragedy. These include: (1) the tragedy of the fatal flaw of *hubris,* in the sense of overreaching (Aristotle); (2) the tragedy of fatally conflicting imperatives or state of being (Hegel) and (3) the special case of Aristotelian tragedy in which fatal flaw and supreme virtue are the same.

Santiago, the hero of the novel is worst kind of unlucky old fisherman, falling down from the eyes of his fellow fishermen. He fell down from the eyes of his fellow fishermen because he was failure in having any catch for eighty-four days. His beginning in the deep-sea makes his rise to the pinnacles of taking the fish more thrilling, the catastrophe of its loss more heartening—and his victory spirit inside and after that catastrophe more life enlarging and transcendent. The tragic action starts in those depth clusters about certain dominant elements. These may be seen as: (1) the magnitude and implicitly ordained quality of the struggle, (2) the heroism of the protagonist in the struggle, (3) the power of the forces arrayed against him and the inevitability of catastrophe once those forces are set in maximum motion and (4) the unalterable options of a great and harmonious order. The presence of Fate is always powerfully felt, but Santiago is never displaced as the generator of his own tragedy.

On eighty-seventh day, he gets a big haul after the struggle of three days, he looks cheerful and feels undefeated, strong enough to catch and pull the huge fish. But his action is against the universal order as he catches the big fish by transgressing his fishing limit and going far off in the sea for it. Consequently, the universal catastrophe comes to him as it comes to all other human beings when they transgress the universal order and are reasonlessly punished by a hostile universe. Santiago acknowledges himself as the author of his own ruin; he knows that he has tried to go beyond the limits of human possibility in making his choices and obeying his imperative, and he knows that he must be punished for it.

The climax of the tragedy reaches and becomes most awesome when marlin jumps and blood comes out. The blood resembles the blood of Christ. Thus, the novel resembles a Christian fable. Marlin thrice circles the boat of Santiago, after the third sunrise, before succumbing to death. The fish is also tragic protagonist in Hegelian concept. After death, also the fish suffers mutilation, which is the final phase of catastrophe and prolongs the catastrophe of Santiago. Santiago feels he has won but fears that he has also lost. He is apprehensive of approaching nemesis "if sharks come, god pity him and me" (37). Sharks do come; they are nemesis. The old man's violation of codes has called them.

Santiago represents all human beings, as does Jesus Christ; his experience is universal human experience, which is tragic. For Hemingway one who has total commitment and dedication to his mission will suffer irreversible catastrophe but will also achieve a spiritual and transcendent victory over it. God exists and man will become a part of him through suffering. Surrounding sea reminds him of his loneliness. Santiago asserts to prove his commitment to his work and reiterates it and kills fish affirming that he is stronger to accomplish his masterwork against all destructive forces, which wrested his prize. Shark's inevitability is not accidental. Catastrophe is pure cause and effect event. Santiago's pride destroys him. When Santiago becomes weak during the course of fishing and pulling the big haul of fish, he invokes the strength of lion and youthfulness of the boy; he dreams of lion and remembers the boy several times during the process. In his soliloquy, Santiago makes clear that he and the fish are incarnations of different states of beings and that each is noble. Each is dominated by single imperative of existence. He reiterates that it was his decision to go far out, to overreach. His equally strong choice is 'not to cut the line.' His choice has been to stay in the deep dark water far out beyond all snares and treacheries:

> My choice was to go there to find him beyond all people. Beyond all people in the world. Now we are joined together and have been since noon and no one to help either of us. Perhaps I should not have been a fisherman... but that was the thing I was born for (26).

Santiago's love for the fish and an almost mystic desire to identify, himself with it, operate simultaneously. The Hegelian imperatives clash external physical entities, but they have now also taken shape inside Santiago's mind as opposing component. They are of a somewhat different shape, as Santiago's love for the fish struggles sadly with his determination to kill it. He is sorry for the fish even as his resolve to kill him remain steady. Because of the fish's 'behavior and great dignity' (41), no one is good enough to eat him. But Santiago's fateful choices have been made, and he stays with them. To quote Writ Williams again:

> The magnitude of the struggle—dimly foreseen at the outset, exploding into shape when the fish strikes and takes command of the boat—is constantly expanding. Aristotle's 'action of a certain magnitude' has been triumphantly established; the old man's daring is going out so far and winning will emerge more and more clearly as Aristotle's fatal flaw after the killing of the fish; his violation of the ordained order then is to receive its inescapable punishment.[16]

Island In The Stream, is the another powerful tragedy that Ernest Hemingway has written. It is the tragedy of Thomas Hudson, a protagonist, painter by profession, who is hammered by the universe. Hudson had achieved the harmony and happiness in both his work and his life. He is secured in both reputation and income, at their highest. But he loses this glory when his two of the three sons are killed in an automobile accident along with their mother, the divorced second wife. His third son dies in Cuba and thus makes Hudson paralytic. Sudden appearance of his first wife who is the true love for him is the gift of consolation in his bereft life but this gift is also snatched away by fate. He finds it difficult to get on with her and the two parts. Hudson has experienced the fluctuating fate. When he is at the peak of joy and power as a painter and is secured in both, reputation and income and when his three sons by his two divorced wives come for an extended visit to him. Hudson fishes, catches a huge fish fighting whole day successfully, and brings the fish to the edge of the boat only to lose him when the hook is dislodged.

Hudson had built the house on the highest level of the narrow tongue of land between the harbor and open sea. This is perhaps the highest achievement, of Hudson for his protection and Safety. But the sea, being universe, is jealous with Hudson's lofty achievements. Hudson is under surveillance of the sea. The sharks, which stay away during day, come closer to his house at night. They are the destructive forces, which would catch Hudson's son and would strike him later.

Suddenly, Roger David appears to Hudson aboard a vessel in harbor. Roger had the record of killing with his fists and is the incarnation of violence. David, Hudson's second son, good natured and loveable, is hit by shark while goggle fishing in the water and is narrowly saved by Eddie, the boat's mate, killing shark with machine gun. Tommy the intellectual and rational son of Hudson acts as coordinator. Andrew, the third son of Hudson, is animalistic in nature. Andrew and Roger are roughly the same substance.

Happy life and happy family are the highest achievements of everybody. Hudson had achieved this but when he learns that David and Andrew have been killed with their mother in a car accident in Europe, his deterioration begins. He feels he has lost part of his own life fabulously. Hudson realizes that Hell is not necessarily as described by Dante or any other great hell describers, but his very once comfortable, pleasant and loving boat. He calls up the strength to continue and make the Journey through hell, which is the manifestation of human condition.

Hudson is again in the grip of hell when the news of his eldest son Tommy's death in Cuba comes to him. He is bereft of human love, forlorn and isolated. He is moving towards catastrophe. His strength and solidity is quickly movingly defined in his encounter with the commander Archer:

> "You don't have to feel cheerful," Fred Archer said.
> "You have got it."
> "You mean, I've had it."
> "You've had it. And you've re-had it. And you've rehad it doubled."
> "Not in spades."
> "Spades won't be any use to you, brother. And you've still got it" (256).

Hudson's first wife, never named, appears in what amounts to a materialization. Through the doorway of the bar, Hudson sees an army-chauffeured car pull to the curb and his former wife steps out. A movie star, she has been entertaining troops on the island and has come looking for him. They move to a renewal of love and even the promise of permanent reunion. But the promise disintegrates in a quarrel and its failure is crystallized in the aborting of a communion ritual; champagne poured is never finished, and eggs prepared are never eaten. Emergency orders summon Hudson back to sea, but the pair has already been forced into an awareness of the impossibility of a permanent return to each other. She has said, "I am tired of you already. We broke up because I got tired of you. You've always loved me and you couldn't help it and you can't help it now" (324). Hudson has reached and lost again and he is now tragic, even though the progress of his tragedy is just becoming clearly visible. He is stripped once more of all the conventional emotional supports and is thus in the vacuum as he moves towards his final action. The defining passage is stated:

> What's one more beating if we get to close? ...get it straight. Your boy you love. Love you lose. Honor has been gone a long time. Duty you do.... Sure and what's your duty? What I said I'd do (326).

Hudson becomes tragic hero, asserting against the Universe, creating with finality, his own definition in the wild. He determines to work even under deepened and intensified anguish and dominated by the approach of death. He resolves to execute his choice in the face of his own death. The hell of pain and loss becomes the part of total complex that threatens to destroy him.

In the face of the loss of his third and last son, and the loss of his only truly loved wife a second time, and of the death he feels approaching to himself he maintains the resolve to perform the function he has chosen and accepted—'his duty.' "That performance is not simply solace but meaning which finally, becomes tragic. The mysterious task that has summoned Hudson and his converted pleasure is to look for wreckage or survivors of a German submarine, which is, sunk northeast of Cuba. After he and his crew discover the nine villagers slaughtered by Germans, and that if he commits himself totally to his orders he and his crew have every chance of being killed; indeed he has recurring premonitions of death. His choice is clear: to interpret his orders discreetly and by no means dishonorably and thus avoid a shooting confrontation and survive-or, to go beyond the minimal necessities of duty, to engage a superior enemy, and thus to risk all the lives in his responsibility, including his own. With complete awareness he chooses, his own death. His extreme commitment moderate what he conceives as his true and necessary course in his collision with the universe is the signature of the largest kind of tragic hero. And in the tradition of magnitude, he feels himself re-conciliated with the cosmos. His deliberate trade of his life for his duty is his transcendence: his devotion to duty is triumph over the physical death.

Hudson now feels himself moving towards death as a result of both, fate and choice, the eternal collusion of tragedy. He is now wounded. He feels he is going to die. His speculation at the dying hours reveals his true character. After he is wounded by the three bullets. Hudson lies down on the deck, taking a last look at the narrow, green banked river, in which the water was brown but clear and the tide was flowing strong.

> He felt away now there were no problems at all. He felt the ship gathering her speed and the lovely throb of her engines against his shoulder blades which rested hard against the boards. He looked up and there was the sky that he had always loved and he looked across the great lagoon that he was quite sure, now, he would never paint and he eased his position a little to lessen the pain. The engines were around three thousand now, he thought, and they came through the deck and into him...the beat of the motor is the beat of life, of universe; it goes into him and he accepts as he accepts that aspect of the sky and sea to which he is witness. He is dying in reconciliation; he has done his utmost and that is his transcendence...his last exchange with Willie suggests, hot at all paradoxically, that the individual is at once part of a loving fraternity, and that he must meet final test, specifically death, with his own isolated fortitude (466).

The Garden of Eden reveals the causes of disintegration of happy marriage of a couple. It is indeed a Garden of Eden in Biblical terms. The hidden power is jealous of their happy life. David Bourne and Catherine spend very happy and pleasant married life. Their mutual devotion and delight in each other at first seem complete and idyllic. Promising David 'a change and surprise.' Catherine cuts her hair short (like a boy's), and begins playing teasing games that hint at exchanging sexual identities. She initiates a friendship with an attractive young woman, Marita and entices David into an amorous 'sharing' of their three lives. Troubled and guilty, he retreats into working intently on a long story about elephant hunting in Africa. Catherine's apparent jealousy of his work precipitates a crisis from which their marriage cannot recover. 'All wicked things start from innocence.' Adam and Eve got the message late and so do David, and Catherine. Her kittenish antics turn savage; she thrusts Marita and her husband together with predictable consequences and then strikes out at both of them. Catherine spoils the Garden of Eden where David lives happily. She is a spoiler whose taste is the forbidden fruit. Thus the novel initiates and completes the Biblical analogy.

David and Catherine spend much of their time in drinking which is the potential source of damage to a creed of writer. He attempts to write his memories of childhood, about the elephant hunting with his father in Africa. This he wants to write as a story. But he is betrayed and Catherine comes in his way. Instead of writing the elephant story she insists him to write about her. She wants him to transcribe into book her body language, which he rejects. This spoils the relationship between the two. Woman is the root cause of this evil. Catherine transforms from sexually docile Eve into caustic and destructive bitch. Her advancing derangement becomes a cause of natural, innocence to fall. In no culture is seen the wife enticing her husband for transsexual relations. This is the flaw in Catherine's personality, which leads to catastrophe. The pleasant garden becomes the cause of the fall of man, and he is expelled from the Garden of Eden.

Catherine is direct descendent of Mrs. Macomber, the woman in *The Short Happy Life of Francis Macomber.* David's meek acceptance of amorous sharing with Marita at the instance of Catherine becomes the fatal flaw consequently brings an agony and disintegration of happy life. The exchange of partners is a threat to the conservation of self. This action leads to disaster.

Catherine desires to be an artist but she has the sense of inadequacy of employment of language, has no confidence in herself because of her gender. Tradition does not permit her to access to the medium of expression of the body, which male can do better and which is easily accepted by society. She creates a text not with language but with her own body.

Catherine wants to translate the body language into proper words. She provides the plot by living it moment by moment. The phallocentric control of letters produces insecurity in the female writer. Catherine believes that the female libido and not written word best expresses reality. She experiences frustration with restrictive gender codes and a sense of powerlessness in the world. She derives both self-respect and sexual satisfaction from communicating with her body—each creative act of self-expression—the hairstyles, the bleaching, the transsexual and bisexual acts manifesting sexual pleasure etc. Catherine clearly speaks a libidinal language and often lets her body express her thoughts, as evidenced when she tells David 'I will put on one of my tight shirts so you can tell what I think about things' (175-76).

Marita and Catherine practice female economy. Both wish to support David but their behavior differs. Catherine's spending is extravaganza unlike Marita. David is not happy about it as he follows male economy. For him money is commodity to be possessed and a signifier of power and sexual control. He equates her spending with her loss of psychosexual dominance and wishes to be free of this perceived debt. Catherine thus transgresses the female role assigned to her by the society. She violates both heterosexual roles and taboos. She demonstrates an attitude, which contrasts vividly with David's. Catherine feels reverence for the ritual of honeymoon while David manifests a desire to adhere to taboos and a tendency to accumulate rather spend... Tired of their criticisms and resistance to her plans, she tells them, you can spend the rest of your lives together...if you don't, bore each other. I have no further need of either of you (191), she soon destroys David's manuscripts in a final, radical effort to ensure work on her own narrative. She never withdraws from her publishing intentions. She says that 'her libido will produce far more radical effects of political and personal changes than some might like to think' (313), and adds that, 'her liberation will modify power relations and bring about a mutation in human relations, in thought, in all praxis' (313). A liberated woman does not use the phallocentric language; rather she invents her own as Catherine tries to do. She wants to break all the barriers of class, gender etc. She obviously wants social change. She is a new woman who challenges male dominated social norms.

Hemingway's work reveals a strong sense of tragedy. His heroes are common men, not men of high rank as Aristotle thought. The Hemingway hero, who is a common man, is equally tragic because his strength and weakness are the same as those of Aristotelian tragic hero. Hemingway belonged to an age in which the common man was the center of actions. All serous writers of his time wrote about this common man—his Joys and sorrows, his disillusionment, and the financial frustration he experienced. The Hemingway hero is a last person whose stoic struggle against the odd circumstances is wreaked in the end. He is the failure before the determining factors against which he fights stoically. However, this lost man is not altogether pessimistic. He is defeated but never crestfallen. He is morally a stronger person. Morality operates predominantly and self-respect are the important traits of the Hemingway hero. He is stoically brave and does not succumb easily to the hostile universal forces. The element of love operates here strongly. The Hemingway hero loses whatever he is committed to. He loves his labour, which is the constant struggle and all the pain and suffering involved therein. Hemingway's vision of tragedy encompasses a larger universe where pain and suffering anticipate a better world to live in. The Hemingway hero suffers vehemently, but he looks forward to a better world. He is basically a morally stronger person who has total faith in himself and the strength with which he offers stiff resistance to the hostile power in the universe. In this sense, he is not really a lost man because in his effort lies the sense of regaining what is lost. The Hemingway hero is the soldier, a bullfighter, a fisherman, known for his physical strength. He is always involved in the violent acts like killing or getting killed. These acts on his part bring out the meaninglessness of violence and cruelty. It is a waste, which creates frustration and the ultimate disillusionment. The death, which is the ultimate result of every action in the Hemingway word, evokes the necessity of love. Love alone will eradicate the pain and suffering associated with labour. Belma Otus has put it better:

> Love is not possible...in a world love and religion are dead. Man must define his moral conditions and live up to them.... Courage, love, humility, solidarity and interdependence—not in supernaturalism and abstraction but hard-won through actual experience in a naturalistic universe which is at best indifferent to man and his values.[17]

REFERENCES

1. S.N. Butcher, *Aristotle's Theory of Poetry and Fine Arts,* with a Critical text and translation of the *Poetics,* with a prefatory essay, *Aristotelian Literary Criticism* by John Gassner, Fourth edition, Dover Publication Inc., 1951, USA, p. 240.
2. Carl J. Friedrich (Edited with an Introduction), *The Philosophy of Hegel,* The Modern Library, 1953-54, New York, p. 80.
3. Wirt Williams, *The Tragic Field and Ernest Hemingway,* Louisiana State University Press, Baton Rouge and London, 1981, p. 133.
4. Ernest Hemingway, *Selected Stories: The Short Happy Life of Francis Macomber,* The Travellors' Library, Jonathan Cape; J. & J. Gray, Edinburgh, 1951, pp. 35-36.
5. Ernest Hemingway, *Essential Hemingway,* including Fiesta (The *Sun Also Rises*), Penguin Books Australia Limited, Ringwood, Victoria, Reprint, 1971, p. 445.
6. Wirt Williams, *The Tragic Art of Ernest Hemingway,* Louisiana State University Press, Baton Rouge and London, 1981, p. 131.
7. Ernest Hemingway, *Essential Hemingway,* including Fiesta (The *Sun Also Rises*), Penguin Books Australia Limited, Ringwood. Victoria, Reprint, 1971, p. 441.
8. Wirt Williams, *The Tragic Art of Ernest Hemingway,* Louisiana State University Press, Baton Rouge and London, 1981, p. 44.
9. *Ibid.*, p. 57.
10. Ernest Hemingway, *Essential Hemingway,* including Fiesta (The *Sun Also Rises*), Penguin Books Australia Limited, Ringwood, Victoria, Reprint, 1971, p. 188.
11. *Ibid.*, p. 189.

12. *Ibid.*, p. 78.
13. Baker Carlos, *Ernest Hemingway's A Farewell to Arms*, included in *The American Novel,* Voice of American Forum Lectures, Popular Prakashan, Bombay, 1967, p. 218.
14. Wirt Williams, *The Tragic Art of Ernest Hemingway,* Louisiana State University Press, Baton Rogue, and London, 1981, p. 165.
15. *Ibid.*, p. 173.
16. *Ibid.*, p. 178.
17. Otus Belma, *The Concept of Death in Ernest Hemingway, Turkey Press, Ankara, 1969, pp. 33, 69.*

5

THE THEME AND THE TECHNIQUE

Hemingway continucs the late 19th century tradition of American novel in a sense that he views man as a helpless victim of circumstances. However, he has no affinity with the Naturalistic technical devices of the late 19th century novel. He adopts Determinism, which is an essential aspect of Naturalism, but as a technical device he disregards it and accepts Realism as a mode of expression.

Naturalism, as a technical device, receives all the details against which man is placed. These details, as naturalist artist believes, are necessary because they determine the fate of the character. This belief dominated the late 19th century fiction, particularly the works of Theodore Drieser and others.

The turn of the century, however, saw different realities. Man's image as a helpless victim of circumstances continued, but a necessity to locate these circumstances in a definite manner was strongly felt. Naturalism, with its association with the Imagination as a creative faculty, allowed personal interpretation of reality. A naturalist artist was a romantic who believed in the idealist notion that beauty lies in not the object but in the eyes of the beholder. Therefore, it offers enormous scope for subjective elements, which hinder the exact and matter-of fact—perception of truth.

20th century, besides other things, was as age of reason. It witnessed scientific advancement, which replaced superstition, with rational view of the world. Reason became an eminent faculty of the human mind with which man made efforts to locate the truth precisely. Imagination no longer dominated the literary creations. Realism became the most important mode of perception and so a major technical device with poets and fiction writers, both in Europe and in America. It became an important mode of expression with the modernist artists on both the sides of the continent, that is, in Europe and in America.

Hemingway is a modernist writer who witnessed and experienced the cruel realities, which the first few decades of 20th century produced at large. He was also influenced by the new scientific spirit, prevailed during his times in the entire West. Therefore, he does not bother about the naturalistic description as the writer of fiction; rather he offers the precise and an exact description of whatever happens. He is a conscious artist who is obvious in his short stories as well as in his novels. His subject matter, by and large, is romantic—he often writes about love—but as a craftsman he is the perfect modernist. He uses language meticulously with every word finally tested. Each of the word he uses is like a Pebble freshly brought from the brook. These words live and shine each in its place. Carlose Baker quotes, Ford Medox Ford in his essay—*Ernest Hemingway's A Farewell to Arms* as saying:

> The words from a less elation, each in order besides the others. It is a very great quality.... The aim—the achievement—of the great prose writer is to use words so that they shall seem new and alive because of their juxtaposition with other words. This gift Hemingway has supremely.[1]

Carlos Baker in the article quoted above offers graphic account of the literary style *of A Farewell to Arms*. He points out that the concluding scene in the novel where Catherine dies and Henry bids a silent farewell before he walks out in the rain was written and rewritten about 32 times till Hemingway was finally satisfied. The silent farewell to the dead Catherine and its impact on the hero is worth quoting:

> 'Is there anything I can do to-night?'
> 'No. There is nothing to do. Can I take you to your hotel?'
> 'No, thank you. I am going to stay here a while.'
> 'I know there is nothing to say. I cannot tell you —'

> 'No,' I said. 'There is nothing to say.'
> 'Good-night,' he said. 'he said.' 'I cannot take you to your hotel?'
> 'No, thank you.'
> 'It was the only thing to do,' he said. 'The operation proved.'[2]

This brief conversation between Henry and the doctor brings out the desired effect. The brevity of the situation and its preciseness brings out the emotional strength felt and experienced by the protagonist.

A Farewell to Arms, is an eminent example of Hemingway's realistic technique. Every word he uses and every sentence written on the page speaks for Hemingway's precise realistic style. The novel is a tragedy resulting out of love's labor, which is lost. This traumatic theme is well brought through a variety of technical devices. Hemingway's concept of life becomes obvious through the technique he adopts for the art of fiction writing. The artist in Hemingway makes himself conspicuous through a variety of natural symbolisms, which sustain and enrich the theme of the novel. Symbolic effects in this novel are achieved through a subtle process of repeated suggestion. The use of weather and the landscape is used symbolically to suggest the gravity of the situation, which is disastrous. Rain is used in the novel as a symbol of calamity, which looms large over the fate of the lovers. The falling rain used as a symbol of imminent doom, the dampness of weather and the eventual rain, which falls in the end, makes the tragic sense complete. When the lovers row across the lake the weather is dark and gloomy and when finally Catherine approaches the time of confinement the rain arrives. The lovers have lived happily in the healthy cold air and clean snow; the cleanliness and healthy atmosphere disappears towards the end of the novel, obviously to suggest that there is something disastrous. It obviously suggests the mortal danger in which Catherine is to be caught.

The symbolic technical device is also used while describing the landscape on which the whole action takes place. There is a carefully established pattern of plains and low lands, which is associated with war, death, pain, sadness, and gloom. On the other hand, the high mountain regions whether in Abruzzi or in Switzerland where the lovers establish temporary peace and are happy and healthy, are associated with pleasure and good life. Thus, the landscapes place the highly suggestive role in the lives of the lovers.

Hemingway uses symbolism as a technical device in other novels as well. *The Old Man and the Sea* offers equally symbolic pattern in which man and the universe confront with each other. The vast sea is the universal force against which a solitary figure of the old man is placed obviously to suggest that man is a tiny creature, which can be crushed by the powerful outer elements. Ironically, the sea also plays a positive role in the life of Santiago. He is away from home and obviously misses the feminine affection. The sea for him thus becomes a woman whom he loves wholeheartedly. The love compels him to stay on the boat even in the face of intimidating factors. His ultimate defeat suggests the tragedy, which is worked out through love and labor. The old man's ceaseless efforts and his willingness to exhaust himself in order to achieve his goal can be compared with the labour of childbirth of Catherine in *A Farewell to Arms*, as there is no way out to Catherine, Santiago is also similarly trapped. He must face the situation because he cannot go back; he must put all his efforts and revive strength in the old delicate body. However, all his labor, like that of Catherine, goes in vain. Hemingway's concept of human tragedy thus is brought out symbolically and to the desired effect in both these novels.

Hemingway's use of symbolism is evident in his short stories as well. *The Hills like White Elephant* suggests the unnecessary burden the protagonist feels as he unwilling to accept the responsibility of fatherhood. *The Cat in the Rain* beautifully brings out the sentiments of a woman through the symbolic presentation of a tiny cat out in the rain. The short story offers an effective picture of modern life in America. It suggests the trend in man-woman relationship, lack of communication between the spouses, and a woman's suffering because of her husband's indifference to her physical needs. The story stands out among others because it reveals Hemingway's concern for the feminine sensibility. The woman in the story is drawn sympathetically. The author obviously shows his concern with the complexities of the female psyche. This is done symbolically as in many other stories in both the volumes.

Hemingway deals with the romantic love in his short stories and novels. This romantic love results in the final tragedy. This is shown symbolically in short stories like *Green Hills of Africa, Death in the Afternoon,* and other. Bullfighting is a display of brutal strength, which is used symbolically as man's recklessness. Hemingway seems to suggest that those who indulge in savage acts like hunting, bullfighting are bound to doom, as indeed they are. Hemingway by displaying the brutality of physical strength also warns against its futility. His favorite theme is war and the favorite conclusion is its destructiveness and brutality.

Ernest Hemingway's technique of writing suggests his refined sensibility. When it is functioning at its highest, it has always worked upon as immediate objective level which translates ideas into terms of concrete things; life as a baseball game where each error is punished by death or compared to the struggle of ants on a burning log, the comparison of a hero's death with the slaughter of animals at a stockyard. In each case there is awareness of double implication, the idea and the image; and the emotional force of the idea is intensified by the shock supplied by the image during Catherine's operation, while the doctor has gone to make his preparations, Frederick is left to administer the anesthesia. He has been told that the correct amount would register upon the dial at number 2, but when Catherine is in extreme pain, he says, "I turned the dial to three and then four. I wished the doctor would come back. I was afraid of the number above two." The use of the machine image suggests Catherine's immediate danger. Another author might have examined in great detail both the Catherine's illness and the emotions, which Frederic experienced at that time; but from the simple quiet statement, reinforced by the dial registering the number above two, the full force of Frederic's terror in few strokes is conveyed.[3]

Hemingway's writing contains fifth dimension effect. He wanted to write and get fifth dimension in his prose and not the ordinary dimension of exposition and description, but full quality dimension of emotional experience, which will give reader the most obvious level of the meaning. *A Farewell to Arms*, the title of the novel points not to the war-arms but the loss of love-arms that Henry suffered. The novel finally suggests that one cannot escape the obligations created out, by his own actions; signing a separate peace will not work and one can not say farewell to arms. One has to live loving people; learn to live with life and learn to tolerate it. Henry's love affair. which blossoms glamorously from the mud of the war, makes him eventually the responsible lover of the humanity.

Earl Rovit in his essay *Learning to Care* observes that Henry initially did not possess a strong potential of caringness. He learnt it in the course of time. He realized that not caring is equivalent to death.[4] Therefore, he ultimately establishes his connection with the world of love, a love affair with Catherine and in doing so, he becomes humanly alive. He accepts the reality of naturalistic world in which death is a fact every bit as real as sex; but he also accepts the reality of a love, which he helped to create, and this fact is also as real as death. And as a final gloss on the novel, there is a small substantiation in the title. A *Farewell to Arms* is beautifully ambiguous in two obvious realms: the farewell to war in the separate peace, the farewell to the beloved in death. But it also suggests a farewell to the world; a farewell to 'not caringness,' which gives a death in life to which no one can resign himself.[5]

Death to Ernest Hemingway is rebirth. Rain as an omen of death at the same time predicts rebirth. Therefore, in his writing the death—rebirth prominently occurs ubiquitously and frequently. Edgar Johnson points out that the separate peace turns out to be impossible if one rejects society and rejects responsibility, he will have to face the cosmic cruelty.[6] Life is only an endless abrasion and destruction. In the opinion of Maxwell Geismar, Hemingway portrays the cumulative degeneration of human temperament under the conditions of war. *A Farewell to Arms* is a series of human defeats. The rain, the cholera, the soldiers who mutilate themselves rather than go on fighting, the growing weariness of the Italian army which led up to Caporatto, the degeneration of Renaldi himself who is sympathetic of the novel's pattern and at its start is so quick. Contrasted against this in turn is the love of Henry and Catherine. Here is another antithesis of increasing joy. The low and the despair are constantly related, intensely intertwined, and in the end almost gain the feeling of life and death themselves, the death preying upon the living organism of the lovers' hope, eating into the flesh and destroying the form from page to page. Yet each change of form, each advance of destruction makes the life in the novel more vital, the life we know must yield, but in the manner of its yielding asserting itself beyond its destruction... struggle to participate in life despite all the odds, from the efforts of the lovers to fulfill themselves in a sterile world, from the exact impact of the human will which Hemingway has negated. Lieutenant Henry turns his back upon our society after Caporatto. Following his personal objectives, he abandons his friends, his responsibilities as an officer, the entire complex of his organized social life represented by the army and the war.[7]

Philip Young in his essay *Loser Take Nothing* observed that Hemingway was not content with his style of writing which had made him already famous. He tries for new effects and does not always succeed. However, the statements that he makes in his writing are impressive and they reveal more than ever could be written out. Philip Young further observed that Hemingway realized and pointed out three years later in *Death in the Afternoon* that love stories do not always end happily in life. Therefore, every story has to be written differently.[8]

Hemingway's writing in fact is not written, according to Wyndham Lewis. It is lifted out of nature and very artfully and adroitly tumbled out upon the page; it is the brute material of every day proletarian speech and feeling, he writes the prose of reality.[9]

His writing represents a pattern of pain and pleasure covering badness and goodness. Many of the reviewers praise *A Farewell to Arms* saying it is a beautiful piece of art. Whereas the critics like Robert Herrick attacks it saying what Wister calls 'garbage' in which Hemingway wraps his pearls.[10] Many of the reviewers and spokespersons of the young generation were willing to admit it as splendid work, chief among them was Henry Sheidel Canby who, in his review says "As for Hemingway's frankness of language, to object it would be priggish. There is no decadence here, no overemphasis on the sexual as a philosophy."[11]

Hemingway's fiction is the works of social redemptive qualities. Though, there seemed to be no political reason to ban *A Farewell to Arms,* Mussolini did it in Italy because it supposedly insulted Military honor and might do damage to national morale.

The mystery where autobiography leaves off and fiction begins has never been solved and is perhaps insolvable according to Bernard Oldsey; how much of Hemingway has entered in his fictional work need to be examined, but in the judgement of critics there is too much of Hemingway in his works. Hemingway fiction has been charged of being too much autobiographical, and there is no denying that some of the Hemingway's work does lend itself to the charge applied indiscriminately to all of his work.

Hemingway was a secular writer searching for religious significance and to find out what is there instead of god. This has been very effectively demonstrated in *The Sun Also Rises* and in the short story *Soldier's Home.* He demonstrates that love of god and the love of a woman could be part of the same religion. 'Marriage' is a psychological advantage. It has a therapeutic solution to loneliness. All Hemingway heroes who are wounded, neurotic, insomniac and afraid of 'dark' the night can be a dreadful time for lonely people once their loneliness has started. But with the Catherine there was almost no difference in the night except that it was an even better time.

Nick Adams has no companionship or love and he has to think either of prayer or woman's arms or alternatively to go for nature's love *i.e.,* fishing. There is no Switzerland of neutrality where one would avoid death and destruction. A careful Hemingway reader would discover that there is not much of Hemingway in his works. Hemingway worked out variations of themes; his work was a continuous process. His forms of literary art demanded that he takes substance from actuality, provided it with mimetic reflection, and produce his own form of combining fiction. Hemingway once described the devised balance for such fiction: "the more the writer learns from experience the more truly he can imagine. If he gets so he can imagine truly enough people will think that the things he relates all really happened and that he is just reporting."[12]

His writing begins with first person plural; something like "we" which signifies we the no-combatants, the onlookers not yet engaged in action (*A Farewell to Arms*), looking across the river and plains to the mountains watching troops and kings going by, hearing that things are going bad and observing what the cholera can accomplish and this "we" reaches to "I" and finally gives way to the protagonist per se like Henry in *A Farewell to Arms.* Sometimes he gives way to "you." Thus, he had adopted the "we" method of narration coupled with poetic method to give powerful effect of fiction.

Hemingway was extremely aware of the craft of fiction writing. He wanted to make a fine craft, which will be realistic. Amending and re-amending his views, concepts, themes and words several times, eliminating some or many of the things he imagined and accepting something different which suits to the work. "Anything you know you can eliminate and it only strengthens your iceberg" was his view.

Hemingway has a definite theme, the subject matter to discuss, a message to convey to the suffering humanity of the modern times America. And he wanted to do it effectively. Therefore, he endeavors to combine the theme and technique, which will produce the desired effect. In *The Sun Also Rises,*

Jake is physically incapable for sexual intercourse. No woman would love such a man in the materialistic and romantic world. Similarly, Brett a young woman who has slept with many men. No one would genuinely love such a morally deranged woman. But Jake loves Brett and Brett is driven closer to Jake than to the physically capable men she knew, despite the fact that he has physical infirmity for sexual satisfaction. Brett is engaged to Mike and becomes widely enamored of Romero, yet these are always recognized, as passing affairs, for it is Jake she really loves.

Hemingway wishes to convey to the world that the god is dead in our time and that the traditional ethical values have become invalid. These are the elements of absurdity in the Hemingway fiction, which make the Hemingway hero akin to the existential hero of Sartre, Camus and Kafka. John Killinger puts it better:

> Hence every man is directed to himself for the formation of new ethics, which will stand in a intimate relation to him alone. And with the tenure of existence limited to this life (without God there is no eternity), aesthetic values are recharged with significance, and are at times virtually equated with ethical values.... To ensure the world freedom, which guarantees individual freedom, the perpetual, hero has been known to join the army in time of war. In doing so, he, like the fictional characters of Sartre and Beauvoir and Camus, swears allegiance to the brotherhood of man and voluntarily suspends his own subjectivity until the freedom of all is assured. But to be externally disciplined is a strain upon him, and he anxiously awaits the dissolution of the fraternity and the moment of his return to the separate peace.[13]

Nevertheless, this man will have to strive hard because the things are not simple and the time is brutal. There is not even lasting love for him. Death being an indiscriminate simplifier, it shears away love with all the other complications of life. Even when a man and woman try to reach an ideal love like the 'I am thee' arrangement of Maria and Robert Jordan, it is interrupted by death. The single Joy left the protagonist in such a world is his pride in the founding of his self through experiences that are genuinely and meaningfully aesthetic and ethical in nature. When no God in heaven, he becomes his own creator, giving form to his own life. Since every man is free to make of himself what he will, his *pundonor* becomes the governor of the extent to which he truly exists. The hero, extremely rigorous with himself, never reaches absolute slothfulness, not even in the case of Harry in *The Snows of Kilimanjaro,* whose honor, long buried under the luxuries brought him by fortune marriages, has goaded him to return to Africa to work the fat off his soul. To say that the novelist glorifies the sensual is to state a half-truth. The whole truth involves an explanation for this apparent glorification, and that, in turn, involves an understanding of Hemingway's thinking about the world....

> ...to learn to live in a world without god and defy the whim willed Setebos of fate; and to learn to live with a self imposed morality and the weak salvation of aesthetics beside the toppled ruin of the religious hope of the age—this for Hemingway, as for Sartre, Beauvoir, Camus, and all the others, is to live authentically in our time. And there is no material more truly heroic than the life that is lived authentically.[14]

Hemingway is a great thinker. The charges that he upholds dominance and superiority, of man over woman are made due to ignorance and due to misunderstanding his philosophy behind fiction. The serious Hemingway scholar will certainly carefully examine the deep-rooted philosophy in his writing for the emancipation of the suffering world. His writing points to the love for the entire suffering world, beyond sensual pleasures. This can be termed as agape—the kind of love often discussed in the Christian context.

The Garden of Eden mirrors the society's ill and suggests transformation in it. It reflects the artistic odyssey of creativity of male and female both in the human society. David Bourne and Catherine both have the quest for artistic creativity and both struggle for its accomplishment. However, the means adopted by them are different and oppose each other. It means that the human society is lopsided tilting more in favor of male and disfavor female. This means discrimination against woman practiced by the male dominated society. Hemingway portraits this truth in his *The Garden of Eden* and the struggle that woman makes to enforce her rights has nothing to do with sexual love that has been interpreted from his writings by his critics.

Catherine goes beyond sexual lust and introduces Marita to her man David something, which appears unconventional. This is done for the benefit of Catherine's man and not for herself. "Griffin suggests that Hemingway was moved by Van Gogh's suffering and sacrifice for the truth and adds, Ernest returned to Paris filled with compassion for the long suffering artist who had wagered his life on his work.... Hemingway showed a similar compassion for Catherine's aesthetic struggle."[15]

Catherine wanted to play a participatory role in the art of David, which is rejected, consequently, she rebels. The imaginary world of his art does exclude her—he is the creator whose creative act seems to replace her own biological function and only his 'narrative' of their life together gives her what she feels is a participatory role. She, in retaliation, becomes creator in the real, unnaturally manipulating life into fictive postures, creating drama. 'I've invited you,' she says of David and Marita, reciprocally trying to control destiny (12). A female text that Catherine wants to create may defy a traditional or phallocentric world. She explains that writing has always been defined by phallocentric laws, and she encourages women 'to write and thus to forge' for themselves 'the antilogous weapon' (312). She explains that women have been indoctrinated to deny their eroticism, hence have been dispossessed of a major source of creativity (312). Cixous says, 'for long time it has been in body that woman have responded to persecution, to the familial conjugal enterprise of dominance, to the repeated attempts at castrating them' (316).

Catherine struggles to control her creative, libidinal urges. However, patriarchal control has profoundly crippled the female psyche. Moreover, the highly creative women suffer from mental diseases or diseases like agoraphobia, anorexia, claustrophobia, etc. Hemingway, therefore, exposes Catherine's sense of insecurity, which often plagues women artists. Woman believes that if she does not behave angel-like, she is a monster. Her nonconformity signals a sort of deviant behaviour. This creates a psychological trauma. Hemingway declares that Catherine's aesthetic insecurities are justified. Not only does David fail to recognize Catherine's artistry, he actually cast them both into traditional roles of domesticity, with Catherine as the passive submissive wife and he himself as the active and suggestive. Catherine consequently desires to perpetuate the free play of the honeymoon in order to delay the closer and restriction of the marital life to come.

Tamara M. Powell is of the view that Hemingway was familiar with Lilith myth through Dante Gabriel Rossetti's poems *Eden Bower* and *Lilith*. This has something to do with *The Garden of Eden*. This perhaps is written in the light of the Jewish creation myth and that Catherine is probably modeled after Lilith who is said to be born at the same time when Adam is born. She prefers to leave the Garden of Eden over the point of disagreement with Adam as to who will be the head of the family and that who will be enjoying supremacy. Lilith not being in agreement with him leaves the paradise and wants to take revenge against Adam. Consequently, she induces Eve to eat forbidden fruit, which is accomplished. However, Hemingway has not wholly painted Lilith in Catherine Bourne. The Lilith legend seems the perfect prototype of *The Garden of Eden,* but the difference between the novel and the myth is that the latter tells the tale with sympathy only for the male, while Hemingway's portrait of Catherine/Lilith is painted with sympathy for the female. Catherine is not a monster. Rather, as he does with so many of his heroines—the wife in *Cat in the Rain,* Jig in *Hills Like White Elephants* and Lady Brett Ashley in *The Sun Also Rises*. Hemingway is fully sympathetic to Catherine. He explores how the conflicting sexual forces with which society pulls at Catherine, coupled with the forces inside her demanding to be heard, ultimately tear her apart.[16]

Hemingway indeed has offered a revolutionary representation of woman in *The Garden of Eden.* This has been done further to show that this revolution in woman will contribute to the advancement of the human society and that woman will love and not hate the man. This is evident from the fact that despite Catherine's anti-conventional behaviour she continues to love him. She tells David, 'No matter if, it's where I've been bad put in how much I love you' (77).

The Garden of Eden shows Hemingway's deep concern for women's suffering. He provides sympathetic portrait of a creative woman, which symbolizes the entire womanhood. He believes that such woman does not victimize man. Hemingway conveys, on the contrary, that there is a need of such woman for the transformation of society we live in equality and liberty of woman will certainly contribute in bringing about the state of praxis in our society. Unless this is accomplished, human society will continue to suffer. Hemingway, therefore, provides an antidote for the ailing society and prescribes agape that is to be followed and practiced for the reconstruction and advancement of human society. Hemingway expects that the male dominated society should realize it sooner for the happiness of every individual human being.

The feeling of futility, terror, and moral degradation born out of war provided themes to several novelists during the period. Ernest Hemingway too handled these themes. Most of his novels exhibit the effects of war and terror and its futility and the moral degradation followed there from. It is observed that Hemingway was deeply influenced by the Freudian psychoanalysis. He offers free and frank discussion of sex for which he was sternly criticized. Nevertheless, what he has exhibited is mostly approved of today. Through his writings, he wanted to bring about the improvement in the society and to set a new tradition in America. His concern for the emancipation of society finally, could point out that one should not find a separate peace but face the challenges posed by the brutal time, have the feelings of agape which is beyond the carnal relations; this alone will bring about emancipation to the degenerated society. However, this task is not simple. In its pursuit, one will have to face great hardships, pay the price of courage and to lay the life too, if necessary. It brings tragedy in such pursuit. "The world breaks everyone and afterwards many are strong at the broken place. But those that will not break it kills."[17]

Ernest Hemingway has written predominantly on romantic view of life. Behind this writing is the concealed purpose; the purpose to seek out the real thing and denounce, expose and parody the established rhetoric and satirized the rosy picture of life. A careful study will reveal that he is preoccupied with certain themes throughout his career of writing. These themes define his vision. The analysis of these themes would reveal that the world is basically chaotic is largely governed by chance. The only firm certainty he finds in this ultimately incomprehensible world is death, which is frequently violent and gratuitous. He also seems to believe that in a death-haunted world, one should live for the moment by refining one's senses through activity as a ritual, which at least imposes a minimum kind of order. One should seek clean, well-lighted, well-ordered place in order to forget the violence of experience.[18] Belief in luck is the only hope to survive in this chaotic world. Otherwise, why should the fiancés of Brett and Catherine die in the war? Why should Jake and Henry get wounded? Why should Kashkin be wounded and Anselmo be killed when they were the most sincere believers in the republican cause? Why should Jordan die and Pablo live? E. Nageswar Rao has put it better:

> These events might not have happened in a world governed by order or justice but because they do happen without apparent order or justice, it becomes futile to see them as other than fortuitous events.[19]

Hemingway believed that the world has certain order; there is God that governs and regulates it and that god disposes what man proposes. Nevertheless, this belief was shaken when he met with the accident in Kansas City and later at the Italian front. He, therefore, emphasized the pervasive role of chance in his world by putting his protagonists in crisis. Human efforts, idealism and will to do good, Hemingway came to believe, get frustrated in such world. In a chance-ridden world love (agape), and labor (struggle) coupled with suffering and death appear the only certainty. All the major characters in his short stories and novels, from Nick Adams, through Henry, Jake, Harry, Santiago, and Cantwell and up to David Bourne of *The Garden of Eden,* struggle for survival and to live peacefully. In a world where human idealism comes of inevitable failure in violence, injury, and death because of the whimsical operations of chance, what can man do? How can any one live in a world, which is governed neither by the logic of the intentional cause and effect nor by divine intent? This is a problem of which Hemingway addresses himself simultaneously with his presentation of a truthful picture *The Way it Was*. His heroes seek means of escaping the specter of traumatic experience, or forgetting the haunting violence, and of avoiding the terror of the enveloping *nada*. If they can neither control chance nor govern their own lives in a chosen way; they have to learn to live with the reality of chance. They realize that only death is certain and that it may come suddenly, violently and undeservedly. The certainty of death and the probable nature of that death make life itself precious to them.

They emphasize living from moment to moment because the next moment they may be gone. In his introduction to *Men at War,* Hemingway states, 'a good soldier does not worry. He knows that nothing happens until then.... Because Hemingway's men live dangerously and because of the uncertainty of their life, they try to compress a full life-span into a few hours or even moments.' In order to escape from the world of violence and chaos amid death they adopt various methods; Nick Adams goes for fishing. In *The Big Two Hearted River.* Jake Barnes takes part in Fiesta in Pamplona, Henry indulges in love, Harry and David, in writing, and so on. Nevertheless, it is not free from danger. It is hard to achieve. People labor and struggle for it. They suffer while seeking life. For them bull ring, trout stream, East African jungles, creative writing, sex etc. are the oasis in the modern chaotic world. These means release their inner tension, fear, hatred etc. This is catharsis in context of the Hemingway tragedy. Nick Adams gets rid of hid tension by writing many things; Francis Macomber feels wild unreasonable happiness; Pablo could sleep like baby after massacre of fascists; Robert Jordan feels purged of Spanish Civil War; Colonel Cantwell gets purged of his war bitterness after narrating his experiences to Renata; and Hemingway himself gets purged when he writes and says that he 'went to Spain to see bullfight and to try to write about them for myself (*Death in the Afternoon*, p. 3). He too felt the need for purging himself of the guilt of killing and fear of death...he felt an inner compulsion to purge himself of these feelings, for, he candidly states in *Green Hills of Africa* 'I must write because if I do not write a certain amount I do not enjoy the rest of my life.'

Hemingway has chosen a new kind of technique to convey his views and influence reader's thinking. This he does through several forms of verbal irony such as parody, sarcasm, understatement, repetition and cyclical pattern etc. Bill Gorton's parody of contemporary moral clichés and the narrator's parody of the hackneyed descriptions of bullfight in *The Undefeated,* illustrates what Hemingway thought was false and hence worthy of his disapproval and discrediting. When Bill Gorton talks of road to hell paved with un-bought stuffed dogs (*The Sun Also Rises*, p. 73), he is indirectly pointing out that the moral language of the past has become inappropriate to the lost generation. In *The Torrents of Spring,* he works to undercut Sherwood Anderson's naive and sentimental attitudes towards love and sex, that reality is different from Anderson's presentation of it in such novels as *Dark Laughter.* Sarcasm which involves an 'inversion of meaning' in that it implies the opposite of what is actually said, is used occasionally by Hemingway to expose what he thought was a distorted view. Frederic Henry's accurate reporting of the battle-police's words to the retreating lieutenant colonel on his patriotic duty is obvious instance where the narrator betrays his sarcastic intention: 'it is because of treachery such as yours that we have lost the fruits of victory' (*A Farewell to Arms,* p. 223). Henry is of course expressing his own bitterness warning us that the attitude of the battle-police deriving from a conventional sense of patriotism and justice is invalid when put to the test of reality. He works to convince us not only that the attitude was wrong but also that its very basis is questionable by evoking contempt for the trite saying through sarcasm and by indirectly drawing our attention to his own authoritative knowledge of the events of the battlefield.

Hemingway uses the Technique of understatement as verbal irony for conveying his vision in which something is deliberately represented as much less, than it really is. At the start of *A Farewell to Arms,* Hemingway, through Henry deliberately makes the understatement:

> At the start of the winter came the permanent rain and with the rain came the cholera. But it was checked and in the end only seven thousand died of it in the army (4).

Although death is not important for soldiers and it does not alarm the soldiers but Hemingway wanted to bring shocks to readers by narrating this manner and the shock underscores the magnitude of the disaster.

Hemingway uses the heroes as examples of the things to be exposed and values to be defended. Nick Adams, Jake Barnes are used to expose the victims' helplessness, insomnia, and unhappy night and thoughts that trouble them. They represent the victims of physical and mental wounds and evoke compassion. Pedro Romero and Robert Wilson are represented for the concentration on perfection in work. Belmonte and Joselito the bullfighters are praised for their *pundonor,* the style and bravery in thee bullring, for bullfighting rather than killing the bull. Nick, Jake, Henry, Jordan are used as war victims and they are used to tell the world at war how the innocent people become the victims and bear the brunt of it; the ordinary people like soldiers, fishermen, bullfighters and all ordinary people suffer and participate in the catastrophe.

Hemingway uses recurring images and repetitions of things and events. Repetition has three concurrent functions in Hemingway's works. It reflects the repetitive patterns in his vision, it shows how deeply Hemingway believed in his vision. More importantly, by using the technique of repetition in a variety of situations and in a number of ways transforms it into a rhetoric instrument. When Hemingway's men and women are trapped under different circumstances in successive novels, when the metaphor of game is repeated in various forms, when the motifs of luck and catharsis recur in almost all his major works, when the circular structure forms the basis of many of his novels, and when the cyclical patter of action is recreated in several works, he uses the means to obtain a better understanding of the world Hemingway has worked with various types of characters in various situations and with different temperaments, but most of them come to the same conclusions about the world. Skilful repetition may be seen in the game metaphor, which recurs in the bullfight, big game hunting and fishing. In all these games, the animal is trapped or cornered, hooked or baited, then killed not through superior strength or courage, but through skill and expertise. The technique of repetition is supplemented by the crucial to an exposition of Hemingway's view. He disputed the contemporary meanings and usage of certain words because these did not, in his view, correspond to contemporary realities. His redefinition of terms like 'morality' and 'defeat' are demonstrated first by dramatized situation and then by exposition. Brett fashions a morality of her own when she was initially infatuated by Romero. She tells Jake 'I don't say it's right. It is right though for me' *(The Sun Also Rises,* p. 184*)*. When she finally, leaves Romero, after deciding not be a bitch who ruins children, her morality becomes for her a substitute for God. The same morality is at work when Cayetano Ruiz, the gambler refuses to divulge the name of his assailant to the police, or when Ole Andreson keeps cool after learning of his impending assassination. This dramatized morality is summarized in his expository work. *Death In The Afternoon:* '*What is moral is* *what you feel good after and what is immoral is what you feel bad after*' (p. 4).

The titles that Hemingway has used in his works are tactical in nature, and are chosen with a calculated verbal strategy. The title *In Our Time* exposes working of the author's mind through ironic contrast of peace implied in the allusion and the violence of the modern time. *The Sun Also Rises* has a biblical origin and indicates Hemingway's considered view of the world in which he wants to convey that no generation is 'lost' but it is a cyclical pattern of the passing of generations in a continuous process, which follow the process of Sun's phenomenon of rising and setting. It suggests the foreshadow of circular journey of the people as represented by Jake and Brett who come back to the same point from where they had began and nothing seems to have been accomplished at the end, Jake remains impotent which symbolizes the condition of the modern man. It also symbolizes the meaninglessness of life for a desperate generation.

The technique of Hemingway's writing kept on changing from time to time. Initially, he used the small sentences of simple nature, which he probably had learnt in his career of journalism. This brought him the fame in the writer's world. With the passage of time and in the later period of his life, he adopted the use of more complex symbolic pattern, abstract words, overstatements, and direct emotional appeal, which made him failure. His pattern of thinking also reflected in his writing. From his works, one can observe that Hemingway has been changing his view from time to time. In the 1920s his views were that 'no country but one's own is worth fighting for,' but two years later he espoused for the Loyalist cause on Spanish Civil War and said 'here is only one form of government what can not produce good writers and that is Fascist system of government, if the war is lost all of those things like equality, liberty, fraternity, personal happiness are lost.' He admired war initially. He believed that war provides opportunity to exhibit one's virility and courage. But he in his later life talked against it and condemned it. He did so when machine replaced man in the war and killed indiscriminately. Initially, he hated women but in his later life supported their cause. In his early career he suggested for the personal comforts but in the later life he realized and said that no single person can make an island of his own and supported the community cause, 'old age softened the hard young man.' This shift in the thinking of Hemingway, reflected very much in his works, made him to write what has not been written before. He himself said in his speech while accepting the Nobel Prize in 1954:

> For a true writer each book should be a new beginning where he tries again for something that is beyond attainment. He should always try for something that has never been done or that others have tried and failed.[20]

Hemingway's writing is closely related to the twentieth century search for values. His idea of love is one such value. However, the idea of love conceived by him, changes. First he writes in reaction to romantic love without quite accepting his own rejection of it. He accepts Eros at all points, in all his works, but eventually he supplements it with agape and finally, sees agape as 'the way out.' There is a chronological development from the first two novels to the period beginning with *Green Hills of Africa* and ending with *For Whom the Bell Tolls*. This middle period is pivotal for Hemingway's love ethics,[21] because he formulated his ideas of love and human involvement in it at this time. These ideas however, changed thoroughly in the course of time. By the time he wrote his last two novels he was a totally different man. Love, he thought, is essential in human life, and this love is a divine inspiration for the suffering humanity. This is a mature version of his earlier days now is transformed into a saintly man who does not bother much about technical formalities. Rather he concerns himself with larger human issues. A kind of deterioration in technical aspect is explicit in later novels like *A Movable Feast,* and *The Garden of Eden*. There is less of violence, more of peace and tranquility, less of individuality, more of human concern. The Biblical myth in *The Garden of Eden* is used not to probe the individual psyche, but is related with women's cause. The Eden garden is a place where Adam exercised his male power over his female companion Lilith—who, in protest, walked out of it.

Thus, there is a continuous growth and development in Hemingway's artistic vision throughout his career as writer. There is, at the same time, a change in his attitude towards form and technique of a novel. He came to believe towards the end of his life and career that the theme and the technique are equally important. There is neither the modernist disregard for the content, nor the sociological obsession with it. And he is not unduly concerned with technical innovation and experimentation as a writer of fiction. That is what distinguishes Hemingway from his contemporary writers both in Europe and in America.

REFERENCES

1. Quoted from *The American Novel, Voice of America,* Forum Lectures, Popular Prakashan, Bombay, 1967, p. 210.
2. Ernest Hemingway. *A Farewell to Arms,* Arrow Books, London, 1994, p. 293.
3. *Ibid.*, p. 286.
4. Earl Rovit, *Learning to Care, ed. Title, Ernest Hemingway,* Twayne Publishers Inc., New York, 1963, pp. 98-106.
5. Jay Gallens (edited by), *Twentieth Century Interpretation of A Farewell to Arms,* A Collection of Critical Essays, Prentice Hall, Inc. Englewood. Cliffs, NJ 1070, p. 40.
6. *Ibid.*, p. 113.
7. *Ibid.*, p. 115.
8. *Ibid.*, p. 131-32.
9. *Ibid.*, p. 86.
10. Older Bernard, *Hemingway's Hidden Craft: the Writing of A Farewell to Arms,* The Pennsylvania State University Press, University Park & London, 1980, p. 7.
11. *Ibid.*, p. 8.
12. *Ibid.*, p. 54.
13. John Killinger, *Hemingway and the Dead Gods: A Study in Existentialism*, University of Kentucky Press, 1960, pp. 98-99.
14. *Ibid.*, pp. 99-101.
15. Kathy Willingham, *Hemingway's The Garden of Eden: Writing with the Body, The Hemingway Review,* Vol. 12. No. 2. Spring, 1993,

The Hemingway Society, University of West Florida, Pensacola, London, p. 49.

16. Tamara M. Powell, *Lilith Started It! Catherine as Lilith in the Garden of Eden.* 1996, pp. 80-87.
17. Uma Tuli, *The Symbolic Technique of Ernest Hemingway,* University of Delhi, 1978, p. 193.
18. E. Nageswara Rao, *Ernest Hemingway: A Study of his Rhetoric,* Hyderabad (ICA), 1980, p. 23.
19. *Ibid.*, p. 28.
20. *Ibid.*, p. 101.
21. Robert W. Lewis Jr., *Hemingway on Love,* University of Texas Press, Austin & London, 1965, p. 6.

6

CONCLUSION

Love and labor constitute a major theme of the Hemingway fiction. It is a theme of the human tragedy as conceived by Hemingway as a writer, which is effectively demonstrated throughout his novels and short stories. Hemingway belongs to an age which is marked by unprecedented violence, unlashed by World War I and other wars across the continent, an age which ushered in an altogether new era. In America, the changes were felt since the late 19th century, particularly after the Civil War. These changes were more strongly experienced during the last decade of 19th century. After the Industrial Revolution the agrarian values disappeared, and the formation of big cities created new problems for the Americans at large. It was a move from rural life to urbanization, to modernization, which is often considered as equivalent to Americanization.

The modern America was more secular and scientific than before. The general worldview prevalent towards the end of 19th century is suggested by the term 'Naturalism.' Naturalism was not only a technical device of fiction writing, but also an attitude, necessarily pessimistic. It was associated with 'Determinism'—a biological theory according to which man is a helpless victim of hostile circumstance often beyond his control. If the nineteenth century Naturalism in America was an outcome of unforeseen changes in society, the twentieth century modernism was the outcome of similar forces. Charles Darwin's Theory of Evolution, the amazing advances in human anthropology demonstrated particularly by Sir James Frazer and Miss Jessie Weston, the analysis of the human mind by Freud and Jung, and above all, the devastation brought about by the First World War—all resulted in an attitude often known as "nihilism" which was an important ingredient of Modernism as a literary concept. Modernism in American literature revealed itself in a variety of manners. In fiction, it is represented by a group of writers known as 'Lost Generation.' These writers had developed a feeling of rootlessness, of being lost from old values and conventions and from the rest of humanity. Ernest Hemingway is a representative of this group of writers in America.

1920s was the decade, which witnessed the culmination of modernist writing in both America and Europe. In America it produced most remarkable writers like Sherwood Anderson, William Faulkner, Katherene Ann Porter, Wallace Stevens, William Carlos Williams, e.e. Cummings, Engen O'Neil etc. These writers, as is evident from their writings, were deeply affected by the outer events, which took place towards the end of nineteenth century as at the beginning of twentieth century and which resulted in the 'modernist' sensibility in arts and literature. This 'modernist sensibility' comes out effectively through the Hemingway fiction.

Hemingway's life is invariably linked with his writings. A writer mostly draws upon his personal experiences, through Hemingway, as a modernist writer of 1920s, would not like to see his personal life directly reflected in his fiction. Nevertheless, there is a definite picture of the life as Hemingway saw it, as he conceived it and loved himself. Hemingway was a lover of life, who relished it in its various manifestations. He was a robust soldier who actively participated in war, and had received wounds as most the protagonists of his novels do. He married four women at different times. This made him know woman closely, see through their vulnerable personalities and depict them in his fiction. There is a general charge against Hemingway that he made his women characters play a secondary role, which the Hemingway hero—the male protagonist-prevailed upon the course of action. To many readers—particularly to the feminist activists, Hemingway's novel *The Old Man and the Sea* is an exercise of male power, as the novel, like Herman Melville's *Moby Dick* is totally devoid of woman character. This view continued till recently.

Most of the scholars considered Hemingway in the modernist context and concluded that Hemingway's world vision is tragic where women's role is mostly negative and fatal. While it is true that Hemingway's world vision is tragic, that he was deeply influenced by the deterministic factors, which were strongly felt after the First World War, it is nonetheless true that he saw women not as performing negative roles in the lives of men, but as their invaluable assets. They share a large portion of the tragedy, which the Heraingway hero experiences and offer meaning and significance to the lonely existence of the man.

Hemingway's concept of human tragedy differs from the classical theory of Aristotle or that of Hegel. He is a product of new times in which the common man came to be valued as much as the classical tragic hero, and the Shakespearean tragic hero of 16th century. The Hemingway hero is a common man—a soldier, a bullfighter, a fisherman, an artist whose genius has deserted him etc. He suffers not as a result of a tragic flaw in his personality, but because he is a victim of circumstances often beyond his control. He is not a creator of these circumstances, but they are imposed on him by the inevitable changes in society and by the other events like war etc. He is caught amid the deterministic forces, which are bent on destroying him. He struggles single-handedly against these forces with courage and stoicism and is ultimately defeated. He meets the tragic end, but reveals remarkable determinism and readiness to struggle for the object he has set his eyes on. This creates a kid of respect for him necessary for a tragic hero. Hemingway has worked out this tragedy through a process, which necessarily involves love and labor.

Nick Adams, the protagonist of Hemingway's short Stories, particularly *In Our Times*, is the initial stage of the making of the Hemingway hero. He experiences and suffers from the torturous reality, which surrounds him. *The Nick Adams Short Stories* are representative of Hemingway's contemporaneity—hence, the title *In Our Times*. The Hemingway hero, as he is called by different names in different novels—Jake Barnes in *The Sun also Rises*, Frederic Henry in *A Farewell to Arms*,

Robert Jordan in *For Whom the Bell Tolls*, Santiago in *The Old Man and the Sea,* David Borne in *The Garden of Eden etc.*—is the prototype of a man who hurls himself out into action and suffers from the consequences. Like his creator, the Hemingway hero is always restless and active. Love for him is a necessary value to live by. It is his faith adopted at a time when religion was reduced down to the level of myth. Love for him is an ideal and a substitute for God. Henry in *A Farewell to Arms* deserts war even at the cost of infamy, because love for him is above everything else. It is love which offers meaning and significance to the crippled life of Jake in *The Sun Also Rises.* Love, which begins as a physical attraction initially, transcends physicality and assumes the form of a spiritual force, which binds the lovers together. The relationship between Jake Barnes and Brett Ashley cannot be described purely as sexual—Jake is incapable of sex—it is that understanding of human beings, which is summed up as "otherness of others." Similarly, the loss of Catherine Barkley is not a loss of sex object to Henry in *A Farewell to Arms*—it is the loss of his personal faith—It is the loss of his own personality. The Hemingway hero, at this stage at least, belongs to the "lost generation" (Hemingway later has denied his association with "lost generation").

The human tragedy in the Hemingway fiction is the result of excessive labor. Love's labor resulting in a loss—that is tragedy. The term "labor" has a vast connotation here. It is pangs of childbirth as in the case of Catherine Barkley in *A Farewell to Arms,* it is an exercise of physical strength to achieve an object as in the case of Santiago in *The Old Man and the Sea.* It is also the emotional strain felt and experienced by Jake Bernes, Robert Jordan, David Bourne even by Nick Adams, the protagonist of *In Our Times.* Such stories as *The Battler, The Three Day Blow, The Big Two-Hearted River*, I, II, etc. demonstrate the shattering experience of Nick which drain him emotionally and physically.

'Labor,' in fact, is an important trait of an active man's personality. The Hemingway hero, who is a man of action, is necessarily involved in labor, which, ironically, leads him towards the tragic end. He is associated with the blistering violence-war, bull-fighting, cesarean with a jack-knife, without anesthesia—are the major features of the Hemingway world. Hemingway's artistic vision, however, is not violent. His protagonists are not engaged in futile exercise of male power as has been generally misunderstood. The artist in Hemingway offers an impersonal view of his contemporary reality, which happens to be what it appears on the surface. Hemingway himself has been in the war, a proof of 'blistering violence'—He has suffered from the evils of war—but there is a difference between the man who suffers and the artist who creates. The Hemingway fiction is a perfect illustration of T.S. Eliot's notion of 'impersonal' art. Therefore, it would be wrong to see in the Hemingway hero the reflection of the writer. By depicting violence and destructiveness Hemingway reveals its futility and devastating impact on the life of an individual and on the society as a whole. The Hemingway hero is always a defeated man, who has undergone a series of traumatic experiences. He is an active witness to the destructive elements, which surrounds him and though he surrenders to them finally, it is only after his stoic resistance to them is over.

Thus, Hemingway asserts the dignity of human efforts—of human labor directed at the object of his love. Love, for the Hemingway hero initially is a physical desire—but gradually it transcends physicality and becomes a universal unifying force for the humanity. It often reaches to that aspect of love suggested by the term "agape"—which is a Christian notion of human welfare carried out through human interaction. "Agape" necessarily involves deep concern for the other's well being through love and affection. It does not involve any sense of selfish worldliness, rather it is a divine feeling aimed at the spiritual upliftment of all. When Henry comes out from the hospital in the war-time Switzerland he is overwhelmed with the feeling of profound loss. His love for Catherine who is dead represents the general sense of ruin, which pervades the whole Europe of the time in which the novel is set. His personal love, thus, assumes the form of a concern for the suffering humanity. The Hemingway hero, who has imbibed the essence of love and who has waded laboriously against the hostile circumstances, projects the concept of human tragedy as envisaged by Hemingway as an artist.

Hemingway's profound literary genius was equally complex and is interpreted in various ways. It is also often misunderstood. For example, he is considered as the one who treated woman as the "second sex"—the one who is inferior to man. The reverse is the truth. If in stories like *Hills Like White Elephants* pregnancy is considered as a liability, it is because men were unwilling to take up responsibility at a time, which had produced several other problems. Again, as in *Cat in the Rain* if women are shown neglected by their male counterparts, the reason is—they are haunted and obsessed by destructive forces, which followed them wherever they went. Hemingway is a realist who depicts the authentic picture of the war-time America—which offered little scope of human intimacy, and when this intimacy was made possible, it led to ultimate defeat and death as in *A Farewell to Arms.*

Hemingway's concern for the woman's cause is evident in his later novels. *The Garden of Eden,* for example, is the story of a woman who has her complete sway over her husband. It is the woman who takes initiatives in matter of love and sex. Catherine, the heroine, initiates another woman in the life of her husband who is a meek, submissive man. The earlier Hemingway is completely transformed in this novel—the one who wrote about hunting, bull-fighting and several unpleasant issues of the war-time America, is concerned here with the strains and delicacies in man-woman relationship. This is true also about other novels like *Islands in the Stream,* which were published posthumously. *The Garden of Eden,* in fact, is used as an image of a woman's revolt against man as is revealed in the Jew's mythology.

The Hemingway fiction is celebrated for its unique style. Hemingway freed the American novel from the descriptive excesses of naturalism, which dominated the late 19th century literature though he continued to be associated with the Deterministic factors of Naturalism as a world-view. Hemingway's artistic vision was formulated by the realities of his own time. There is a considerable influence of the modern thinkers like Freud, Einstein and others on the Hemingway fiction. Frederick Henry in *A Farewell to Arms* reveals his acute consciousness of time as the lovers elope secretly and unguarded. He recites those famous lines from Marvell's *To His Coy Mistress,* which have become the emblem of the modernist consciousness of time:

> and always at my back, I hear,
> Times winged chariot hurrying near (p. 122).

Hemingway was also influenced by such literary movements like Symbolism, Imagism etc., which were important aspects of the 20th century modernism. He makes extensive use of symbols and images in novels like *A Farewell to Arms, The Sun Also Rises,* and *The Old Man and the Sea.* The effective use of ancient myths can be traced in novels like *For Whom the Bell Tolls, The Garden of Eden.* The use of symbols and images results into that economy of language for which the Hemingway fiction is praised by critics unanimously. Hemingway was always down-to-earth when he wrote about the worldly things. His style has tremendous appeal for those who have suffered from the hostility of the world. Ralph Ellison, the famous African-American novelist of 1950's, wrote in one of the essays collected in *Shadow and Act*:

> Do you still ask why Hemingway was more important to me then Wright? Not because he was white or more into "accepted." But because he appreciated the things of this earth which I love and which Wright was too driven or deprived or inexperienced to know, weather, guns, dogs, horses, love and hate and impossible circumstances which to the courageous and dedicated could be turned into benefits and victorious. Because he wrote with such precision about the process and technique about the daily living that I could keep myself and brother alive during the 1937 Recession

> by following his description of wing-shooting; because he knew the difference between politics and art and something of their true relationship for the writer. Because all he wrote—and this is very important was imbued with a sprit beyond the tragic with which I could feel at home, for it is very close to the feeling of the blues, which are perhaps as close as American can come to expressing the spirit of tragedy.[1]

It sounds paradoxical that Hemingway who wrote of love as a feeling that binds human souls has the most worldly style. His characters are the inhabitants of the earth, when the earth was a victim of man-made atrocities. The sufferings of the earth appealed men like Ralph Ellison—who was a victim of man-made custom of slavery in America. The human tragedy, which emerges as a prominent theme in the Hemingway fiction, is conveyed in a style, which is down-to-earth, so that its human factor is prominently stated. Thus, Hemingway's style of fiction writing is an effective device to demonstrate the theme of human tragedy caused by love's tabor, lost in the case of the Hemingway hero.

The conclusion arrived at after the thorough analysis of Ernest Hemingway's major novels and short-stories in the light of the theme of this study, can be stated as follows:

1. Hemingway wrote at a time when the entire West was struggling to recover from the cultural blows it received at the end of 19th century and in the beginning of the twentieth century. It was a transitory time when a generation of sensitive young writer found it difficult to catch up with.
2. Of all the events to affect Hemingway's creative sensibility was war. May be because he actively participated in the World War I as a wartime correspondent and as ambulance driver, and had also received serious injuries.
3. Besides war, Hemingway writes extensively of love. Love stories set against the destruction of war often end in tragedy. The Hemingway hero is essentially a tragic hero. Hemingway's concept in a sense that the

Hemingway hero is always a common man, and is the victim of outer circumstances, rather than of the flaw in his own personality.

4. Love is the basic cause of the tragedy of the Hemingway hero. Love for him is an alternate God, a faith which he wants to adopt in place of the lost values of his times. This love begins as an attraction for the opposite sex, and in the course of time, transcends physicality. It assumes the form of a divine feeling often expressed by the term 'agape.'
5. With love is associated labor—the ceaseless effort to win over the hostile circumstances. The continuous struggle on part of the Hemingway hero exhausts him emotionally as well as physically resulting ultimately in the tragic end. The stoic resistance the Hemingway hero puts against the universal hostility raises his stature in the eyes of the reader. His tragedy is as concerning as that of King Oedipus, King Lear, or of Hamlet, the Prince of Denmark.

Thus, love and labor are the basic ingredients of the theme of human tragedy in the Hemingway fiction.

REFERENCE

1. Quoted from Introduction to Hemingway's last novel *True At First Light,* edited by Patrick Hemingway & Bozeman Montana, William Hermann, London, 1999, pp. 10-11.

BIBLIOGRAPHY

Primary Sources

Novels by Ernest Hemingway

The Torrents of Spring. Charles Scribner's Sons, New York, 1926.

The Sun Also Rises. Charles Scribner's Sons, New York, 1926.

A Farewell to Arms. Charles Scribner's Sons, New York, 1929.

Death in the Afternoon. Charles Scribner's Sons, New York, 1933.

Green Hills of Africa. Charles Scribner's Sons, New York, 1935.

To Have and Have Not. Charles Scribner's Sons, New York, 1937.

For Whom the Bell Tolls. Charles Scribner's Sons, New York, 1942.

Across the River and into the Trees. Charles Scribner's Sons, New York, 1950.

The Old Man and the Sea. Charles Scribner's Sons, New York, 1952.

Island in the Stream. Charles Scribner's Sons, New York, 1970.

The Garden of Eden. Hamish Hamilton, London, 1986.

True At First Light. (Ed.) Patrick Hemingway & Bozeman Montana, William Hermann, London, 1999.

Short Stories by Ernest Hemingway

In Our Time. Boni and Liveright, New York, 1925.

Man Without Women. All Listed under *The Fifth Column and the First*.

Forty-nine Stories. Charles Scribner's Sons, New York, 1938.

Winner Take Nothing. Charles Scribner's Sons, New York, 1933.

Men at War (Anthology). Crown Publishers, New York, 1942.

The Snows of Kilimanjaro and other Stories. Charles Scribner's Sons, New York, 1961.

Movable Feast. Charles Scribner's Sons, New York, 1964.

Secondary Sources

Critical Books, Articles etc. on Hemingway's Fiction

Abraham, T.V., *Ernest Hemingway: A Study of The Concept of Victory in His Fiction and Short Stories*, Nagpur, 1994.

Aldridge, John W., *After The Lost Generation: A Critical Study of the Writers of Two Wars*, NY: Mc. Graw-Hill Book Company Inc., 1951.

Arora, Vishwa Nath, *Search for Identity in the Novels and Short Stories of Ernest Hemingway*, Chandigarh, 1971.

Banerjee, Anupa, *Portrait of the Artist in Hemingway's Fiction*, Kurukshetra, 1992.

Belma, Otus, *The Concept of Death in Ernest Hemingway*, Turkey Press, Ankara, 1969.

Bigsley, CWE, *Hemingway, The Recoil from History: In The Twenties*. Ed. Warren French, 1922.

Brooks, Cleanth, *The Hidden God: Studies in Hemingway*, Faulkner, Yeats, Elliot and Warren, New Haven, Yale University Press, 1963.

Butcher, S.N., *Aristotle's Theory of Poetry and Fine Art With a Critical Text and Translation of the Poetics, with a Prefatory Essay*, Aristotelian *Literary Criticism by John Gassner*, Fourth Ed., USA: Dover Publication Inc., 1951.

Carlos, Baker, *Ernest Hemingway: Critiques of Four Major Novels*. New York. Charles Scribner's sons, 1962.

Carlos, Baker, *Hemingway, The Writer As Artist*, Princeton, NJ: Princeton University Press, 1972.

Chandra Sekhara, Raju G. *The Apocalyptic Vision of the 'Lost Generation' With Special Reference to Fitzgerald and Hemingway,* Tiruchirapalli, 1993.

Cooper, Stephen, *The Politics of Ernest Hemingway,* Ann Arbor, Mich: Umi Research Press, 1987.

Dahiya, Bhim S., *Hemingway's The Sun also Rises: Critical Introduction,* Lakesid Publisher, New Delhi, 1986.

Dalal, B.P., *Glimpses of American History,* Vol. II, Vora and Company, Bombay, 1981.

Das, Satyabrata, *Ernest Hemingway: The Turning Point,* Atlantic Publishers & Distributors, New Delhi, 1996.

Dimri, Jaiwanti, *The War and the Wound, Ernest Hemingway's Short Stories and Non-fiction,* Meerut, 1980.

Donna, Krolic Hollenberg H.D., *The Poetics of Childbirth and Creativity,* Northeastern University Press, Bostton, 1991.

Donaldon, Scott (ed.), *New Essays on a Farewell to Arms,* Cambridge University Press, New York, 1990.

Encyclopedia of Religion, Vol. 9, Long, J Bruce, "LOVE," Macmillan and Free Press, Macmillan Publishing Company, New York, 1987.

Fielder, Leslie A., *Love and Death in the American Novel,* Third Scanborough Book Edition, New York 10510, 1982.

Fisher, William J.H., Willard Reniger, Ralph Samuelson, K.B. Vaid (ed.), *American Literature of the Nineteenth Century, An Anthology,* Eurasia Publishing House (Pvt.) Ltd., reprinted, New Delhi, 1983.

Fisher, William J., *Hemingway's Tragedy of the Common Man* (Reprinted from SPAN), March 1962.

Fraiberg, Louis, *Psychoanalysis And American Literary Criticism,* Detroit: Wayne State University Press, 1960.

Frazer, G.S., *The Modem Writer and His World,* Harmondaworth, England: Penguin Books Ltd., Middlesex, England, 1979.

Friedrich, Carl J., (edited with an Introduction), *The Philosophy of Hegel,* The Modern Library, New York, 1953-54.

Garg, Vandana, *Hemingway And Human Suffering: A Study of for Whom the Bell Tolls, Old Man and the Sea, Island in the Stream,* Kurukshetra University, Kurukshetra, 1981.

Gerry, Brannar, *Concealment in Hemingway's Works,* Columbus, Ohio State University Press, 1983.

Gellens, Jay (ed.), *Twentieth Century Interpretation of a Farewell to Arms: A Collection of Critical Essays,* Englewood Cliffs, Prentice Hall, NJ, 1970.

Glickberg, Charles I, *The Sexual Revolution in Modern American Literature,* Martinus Nijheff/The Hague, 1971.

Grebstein, Sheldon N. Comp., *Merrill Studies in For Whom the Bell Tolls*. Columbus, Ohio, Merrill, 1971.

Grimes, Larry E., *The Religious Design of Hemingway's Early Fiction,* Ann Arbor, *Umi* Research Press, Mich, 1974.

Griffin, Peter, *Along with Youth: Hemingway, The Early Years.* Oxford University Press, New York, 1985.

Gupta, Das Hemendralal, *Hemingway: Expatriate in Search of Life in Europe,* Kharagpur, 1974.

Gurko, Leo, *Ernest Hemingway and the Pursuit of Heroism,* Craw Well, New York, 1968.

Guttmann, Allen, *The Wound in the Heart: America and the Spanish Civil War*, Free Press of Glencae, New York, 1962.

Hays, Peter L., *Ernest Hemingway,* The Continuum Publishing Company, New York, 1990.

Heiney, Donald, *Recent American Literature After 1930, in Barron's Educational Series,* ed. Downs Lenthiel H. Woodburg, New York, 1974.

Hoffman, Fredrick J., *The Twenties: American Writings in the Post War Decade,* The Viking Press, New York, 1955.

Hofstadler, Richard, *The Age of Reform: from Bryan to F.D.R.,* Jonathan Cape, 30 Bedford Square, London, 1962.

Hunt, George W. SJ., *John Updike and the Three Great Secrets: Sex, Religion and Art,* Grand Rapids. William B. Eerdman Publishing Company, 1980.

Jain, Satya Prakash, *Short Stories of Ernest Hemingway, Study in Meanings,* Delhi, 1976.

Jobes, Katherine T. (ed.), *Twentieth Century Interpretation of the Old Man and the Sea: A Collection of Critical Essays,* Englewood Cliffs, Prentice Hall, NJ, 1968.

Johnston, Kenneth G., *The Tip of the Iceberg: Hemingway and the Short Story,* Greenwood, Fla., Penkeville Publishing Co., 1987.

Joseph, Warren Beach, *American Fiction*, 1920-1940, Russell, New York, 1960.

Keniston, Kenneth, *The Uncommitted: Alienated Youth in American Society,* Dell Publishing Company, NY, 1960.

Killinger, John, *Hemingway and Dead Gods, A Study in Existentialism,* University of Kentucky Press, 1960.

Lawrence R., Broer, *Hemingway's Spanish Tragedy,* University of Alabama Press, 1973.

Lee, Robert A. (ed.), *Ernest Hemingway:* New *Critical Essays, Vision,* Totowa, NJ, 1983.

Lewis, Robert W. Jr., *Hemingway on Love,* University of Texas Press, Austin & London, 1965.

Lillian, Ross, *Portrait of Hemingway.* Avon, New York, 1961.

Lincoln, Kenneth, Native *American Renaissance,* University of California Press, Berkley, 1983.

Link, Arthur S. & William B. Cotton, *American Epoch, A History of the United States Since* 1900. Vol. The Progressive Era and the First World War 1900-1920, Alfred A. Knopf, NY.

Luccock, Halford *American Mirror, Social, Ethical and Religious Aspects of American Literature,* 1930-40.

Loren, Baritz. *The Culture of the Twenties,* New York and London: McMilan, 1985 (First published in 1970).

Mangathayaru, G.A., *The Theme of War in the Novels of Ernest Hemingway with Special Reference to The Sun also Rises, A Farewell to Arms, and For Whom the Bell Tolls,* Guntur, 1989.

Mark, Twain, *The Adventures of Huckleberry Finn.*, Tom Doherty Associates, Inc., New York, 1985.

Mathur, U.S. *Ernest Hemingway: A Farewell to Arms,* Arti Book Center, New Delhi, 1981.

Mc. Carmick, John. *American Literature* 1919-1932*: A Comparative History,* Routledge & Kegan Paul, London, 1971.

Meyers, Jeffrey (ed.), *Hemingway the Critical Heritage,* Routledge & Kegan Paul, London, 1982.

Meyers, Jeffrey, *Hemingway: A Biography,* Harper & Row, New York, 1985.

Micheal, Ordent, *What is Behind Love? Oxytocin, In Gardian, London,* News article in *Indian Express,* February 15, Mumbai, 1999.

Michael, Perman, *Perspective of the American Past, Reading and Commentary on Issues in American History,* Vol. Two, 1865 to the Present, University of Illinois at Chicago Scott, Foresman and Company.

Mishra, Ajit Kumar, *Theme of Loneliness in Modern American Fiction,* With Special Reference to Sherwood Anderson, Ernest Hemingway and Thomas Worlfe, Bhagalpur, 1977.

Mitsutomi, Shogo, *Cubistic structure in the Prose of Ernest Hemingway, Kyushu American Literature,* Vol. 38, Dec. Japan, 1997.

Mundra, S.C., Ernest *Hemingway, The Impact of War on His Life and Works.* Prakash Book Depot, 1988.

Nair, Ramchadra N., *Critical Study of the Thematic and Formalistic Anticipations of the Later Hemingway as seen in his Early Writings,* Calicut, 1979.

Nesbet, Robert, *The Present Age, Progress And Anarchy In Modern America,* (first ed.), Harper and Row, New York, 1988.

Nobel, Donald R. (ed.), *Hemingway, A Revolution Troy,* Whitston Publishing Company, New York, 1983.

Oldsey, Bernard, *Hemingway's Hidden Craft, The Writing of A Farewell to Arms.* University Park & London: The Pennsylvania State University Press, 1980.

Oliver, Egbert S., *American Literature* 1890-1965, *An Anthology,* Eurasia Publishing House (Pvt.) Ltd., reprinted, New Delhi, 1983.

Otis W. Coan. and Richard G. Lillard, *America in Fiction: An Annotated list of Novels that Interpret Aspects of Life in the United States, Canada, and Mexico,* 5th ed. California: Pacific Books, Publishers Palo Alto, 1967.

Pagey, Sulabha, *Ernest Hemingway: Interpretation of the Themes of His Novels,* Ujjain, 1974.

Paul, Sukrita, *Man-Woman Relationship in the Fiction of F. Scott Fitzgerald, Ernest Hemingway and Theodore Dreiser,* Aurangabad, 1975.

Paul, Sukrita, *Man, Woman And Androgyny: Study of the Novels of Theodore Dreiser, Scott Fitzgerald and Ernest Hemingway,* Indus Publishing Company, New Delhi, 1989.

Presley, John W., *Hemingway Notes,* Vol. 3, No. 1, Caslisle, Spring, Pennsylvania, 1973.

Raeburn, John, *Fame Became of Him: Hemingway as Public Writer,* Indiana University Press, Bloomington, 1984.

Rajyalakshmi, *War Novels of Hemingway: A Study,* Visahapatanam, 1991.

Rao, Nageswara E., *Ernest Hemingway: A Study of His Rhetoric,* New Delhi: Arnold Heinmann, 1983.

Rao, Rama P.G., *Narrative Technique of Ernest Hemingway,* Bhubaneswar, 1970.

Rao, Rama P.G., *Ernest Hemingway: Study in Narrative Technique,* S. Chand, New Delhi, 1980.

Raymond, Nelson S., *Ernest Hemingway Life, Work and Criticism,* York Press Ltd., Canada, 1984.

Reinhold, Niebuhr, *The Irony of American History,* Charles Scribner's Sons, New York, 1952.

Reynalds, Michael S., *The Young Hemingway,* Basil Blackwell, New York, 1986.

Reynolds, Michael S., *The Sun Also Rises, A Novel of the Twenties,* Twayne Publishers, Boston, 1988.

Reynolds, Michael S., *Critical Essays on Ernest Hemingway's In Our Time,* Mass. G.K. All & Co., Boston, 1983.

Rosen, Kenneth Mark, *Ernest Hemingway: The Function of Violence,* Ann Arbor: University, Microfilms International, 1969.

Rovit, Earl H., *Ernest Hemingway,* Twayne Publishers, New York, 1963.

Rudat, Wolfgang E.H., *A Rotten Way to be Wounded: The Tragicomedy of The Sun Also Rises.* Peter Long Publishing, Inc., NY, 1990.

Sanderson, Rena, ed. *Blowing the Bridge, Essays on Hemingway and For Whom the Bell Tolls,* Greenwood Press, New York, 1992.

Scafella, Frank [ed.], *Hemingway: Essays of Reassessment,* Oxford University Press, 1991.

Scott, Donaldson, *Towards a Definitive Biography,* Oxford University Press, 1991.

Scott, Donaldson, *By Force of Will: The Life and Art of Ernest Hemingway,* Viking Press, New York, 1977.

Scott, Wilbur S., *Five Approaches of Literatary Criticism, an Arrangement of Contemporary Critical Essays,* Seventh Printing, Collier Books, A Division of Macmillan Publishing Company, Inc., New York, 1974.

Sharma, Dilbagh Rai, *Ernest Hemingway: His Consciousness of Human Predicament,* Punjab University, Chandigarh, 1968.

Sharma, Dilbagh Rai, *Empirical Ethics of Ernest Hemingway,* Chandigarh, 1969.

Sharmah, Narayan, *Ernest Hemingway: A Critical Study of His Novels with Special Reference to His Treatment to Love* (Thesis), Meerat University, Meerat, 1974.

Singh, Chandel Surendra, *Violence in Hemingway,* Printwell Publishers, Jaipur, 1991.

Singh, Jaspal, *Semiotic Analysis of Hemingway's The Old Man and The Sea,* Bahri Publications, New Delhi, 1990.

Singh, Sukhbir, *The Survivor in Contemporary American Fiction,* New World Literature Series: 31, B.R. Publishing Corporation, Delhi, 1991.

Smith, Carol H., *Women and the Loss of Eden in Hemingway's Mythology, In Ernest Hemingway: The Writer in Context,* Ed., Nagel, and James, Madison, Wisconsin: University of Wisconsin Press, 1984.

Srivastava, Ramesh Kumar, *Determinism in Hemingway,* Guru Nanak Dev University, Amritsar, 1975.

Srivastava Ramesh Kumar, *Hemingway and his For Whom The Bell Tolls.* Guru Nanak Dev University, Amritsar, 1980.

Sundararajan, R., *Impact of War on Hemingway with special reference to A Farewell To Arms, and For Whom the Bell* Tolls. Madras, 1987.

Syed, Ali Hamid, *Short Fiction of Ernest Hemingway: Study in Major Themes.* Lucknow, 1980.

Syed, Ali Hamid, *Short Fiction of Ernest Hemingway: Study in Major Themes,* Asia Publishing house, New Delhi, 1985.

The Holy Bible, New International Version containing The Old Testament and The New Testament. Eccles, 7: 26, Zondervan Bible Publishers, Grand rapids, Sixth Printing, Michigan, February, 1987.

Tetlow, Vendolyn E., *Hemingway's In Our Time, Lyrical Dimensions,* Bucknall University Press, Lewinsburg, 1992.

Tripathi, J.P., *Ernest Hemingway: A Study in his Evolution,* first ed., Prakash Book depot, Bareilly, 1990.

Tuli, Uma, *The Symbolic Technique of Ernest Hemingway* (Thesis), University of Delhi, Delhi, 1978.

Van O'Connor, William Ed. *Seven Modern American Novelists : An Introduction,* Popular Prakashan, Bombay, 1968.

Villard, Henry S., and James Nagel, *Hemingway In Love and War, Last Diary of Agnes Kurowsky, her Letters and Correspondence of Ernest Hemingway,* Northern University Press, Boston, 1989.

Von Kurowsky, Agnes, Viler, Henry Serrano, Nagel, James JT. (ed). *Hemingway In Love and War: The Last Diary of Agnes Von Kurowsky, Her Letters and Correspondence of Ernest Hemingway,* Northeastern University Press, Boston, 1989.

Waldhorn, Arthur, *A Reader's Guide To Ernest Hemingway,* Farrar, 1972.

Waldhorn, Arthur Comp., *Ernest Hemingway: A Collection of Criticism,* New York: Macgraw-Hill, 1973.

Walter, Allen, *Tradition and Dream,* A Critical Survey of British and American Fiction, From 1920s To The Present Day.

Wagner-Martin, Linda, (ed.), *New Essays on the Sun Also Rises,* Cambridge University Press, Cambridge, 1987.

Weaver, Gorden, (ed.), *American Short Story* 1945-1980, *A Critical History,* Oklahoma State Union, Twayne Publishers, 70, Lincoln Street, Boston, Massachusetts 0211, 1983.

Weeks, Robert P., (ed), *Hemingway, A Collection of Critical Essays.* Englewood Cliffs, Prentice Hall, Inc., N.J.

White, William, *Merrill Studies in the Sun also Rises, Columbus,* 1969.

Whitlow, Roser, *Cassandra's Daughters: The Women in Hemingway,* Westport, Conn., Greenwood Press, 1984.

Wilson, Christopher P., *Labor of Words: Literary Professionalism in the Progressive Era,* MASS: Auth The Author, Boston, 1983.

Wilson, Edmund, *The Wound and the Bow, Seven Studies in Literature,* Oxford University Press, New York, 1965.

Young, Philip, *Ernest Hemingway,* Minneapolis: University of Minnesota Press, 1959.

Young, Phillip, *Hemingway, and the Image of Man, A Review,* Partisan Review, May-June, 1953.

Journals/Research Papers and Magazines

Encyclopedia of Religion, Vol. IX, Raymond Fogelson D. "LOVE," New York: Macmillan and Free Press, Macmillan Publishing Company, Collier Macmillan Publishers, London, 1987.

Encyclopedia of Religion, Vol. 3, Demetrios, J. Constantelos, "CHARITY", Mac million and Free Press, Macmillan Publishing Company, London: Collier Macmillan Publishers, New York, 1987.

The American Review, Vol. 31, University of West Florida, Pensacola, Florida, 1987.

The American Review, Vol. 31, Ward Just, "A Code for the Twentieth Century," 1987.

The Hemingway Review, Vol. 6, No. 1, Hemingway Society, University of West Florida, Pensacola, Florida, Spring, 1986.

The Hemingway Review, Vol. XI, No. 2, Culver, Micheal, "The Spring in the Dark, Hemingway's Strater and the Old Man in the Sea," Hemingway Society, University of West Florida, Pensacola, Florida, Spring, 1992.

The Hemingway Review, Vol. 12, No. 2 Hemingway Society, University of West Florida, Pensacola, Florida, Spring 1993.

The Hemingway Review, Vol. 12, No. 2, Mare, Dolan. *The Good Writer's Tale: The Fictional Method of Hemingway's Scott Fitzgerald,* Spring 1993.

The Hemingway Review. Vol. 16, No. 1, Ryan, Dannis, "A Divine Gesture, Hemingway's Complex Parody of the Modern," Hemingway Society, University of West Florida, Pensacola, Florida, Fall, 1986.

The Hemingway Review, Vol. 11, No. 1, Hannum, Howard L., "Jig Jig to Dirty Years," Fall, 1991.

The Hemingway Review, Vol. 12, No. 2, Willingham Kathy, "*Hemingway's The Garden of Eden. Writing with the Body.*" Spring, 1993.

The Hemingway Review, Robert, Solotaroff, "Sexual Identity in A Farewell to Arms," Vol. 9, No. 1, Hemingway Society, University of West Florida, Pensacola, Florida, Fall, 1989.

The Hemingway Review, Vol. 15, No. 2, spring, 1996, Powell, Tamara *M. Lilith Started It! Catherine as Lilith in the Garden of Eden.* Spring, Pennsylvania, 1996.

The Hemingway Review, Vol. 17, No. 1, Fall, Marsell, Darrel, "Words *Lost in Our Time,*" 1997.

Indian Journal For American Studies, Vol. 26, No. 1, 'Winter,' ASRC, Hyderabad, 1996.

Modern Fiction Studies, Vol. 20, No. 4, Quarterly, Department of English, Purdue university, West Lafayette, Indiana 47907 Winter, 1980-81.

The New Yorker, Lillian Ross, *Hemingway Told Me Things, Notes on A Decade's Correspondence,* May 1999.

Hemingway Woman and Sexual Politics Nirmal Mukharji's Research Paper-unpublished.

The Southern Review, Essays and Reviews, Vol. 35, No. 2, Spring, Louisiana State University at Baton Rouge. Louisiana, 70803, 1999.

The Times of India, Mumbai, April 20, 1999.

The Voice of America (VOA), The American Novel, Forum Lectures, Popular Prakashan, Bombay, 1967.

INDEX

V

W

Z